Red, White, and Blue: The Issue

Franklin E. Rutledge

Bloomington, IN  Milton Keynes, UK

authorHOUSE®

AuthorHouse™
1663 Liberty Drive, Suite 200
Bloomington, IN 47403
www.authorhouse.com
Phone: 1-800-839-8640

AuthorHouse™ UK Ltd.
500 Avebury Boulevard
Central Milton Keynes, MK9 2BE
www.authorhouse.co.uk
Phone: 08001974150

First published by AuthorHouse 6/19/2007

ISBN: 978-1-4259-9744-1 (sc)

Library of Congress Control Number: 2007901380

Printed in the United States of America
Bloomington, Indiana

This book is printed on acid-free paper.

Foreword

"This is a very thought-provoking piece that reveals to us the true spirit of America, and causes us to realize the significance of this country's place in the world. One must read this book for themselves to appreciate the revelatory knowledge imparted unto its author; for although he has invested a substantial amount of time researching his topic, it could only be by the divine inspiration of God that one could obtain such an interesting perspective on ancient and modern world history. In fact, this is a must read for history buffs, and Bible scholars alike!"

Bishop Theodore L. Brooks Sr.,
Founder, T.L. Brooks Ministries
Pastor, Beulah Heights First Pentecostal Church
(New Haven, CT)

Franklin Rutledge is a dear friend with wisdom well beyond his years. We were classmates in the 70's and grew up in the middle of Alabama. Integration came to our town in 1971. Our class was unique because we loved and respected each other regardless of our skin color. He is one of those rare individuals that can look at people, and not see color. I believe his book will help Americans acquire that same attitude.

He shows us that we can disagree with someone, but still love and respect them for who they are. Forgiveness is the reason he is able to be prosperous and to pursue his definition of happiness. He is changing the world with his example of sincerely loving and forgiving others, showing respect to his flag and country, and to the Lord. I am proud of his accomplishments as a writer, minister, mentor and friend! I speak for the entire Class of 1977, and say that we are all proud of him.

This book reveals that God ordained the conception and birth of this country. God desired a country that would bring the world back to Christ. This book, if read with an open mind, will help us understand exactly how he did it.

Most Americans dream of living in a country of diverse people who can live together showing respect for each other, respect for the flag which represents this ordained country, and to God. This book teaches us how to pledge allegiance to God, and to this country, so that we can have the harmony of a diverse nation.

If we are in God's will today, we had to come through someone that was in the will of God yesterday. The brutal treatment of the American Slaves, the Indians and the suppression that women were inflicted upon were by the hand of man, not God. Many of us came to America by the divine providence of God. For the sake of personal and continental wealth and happiness, we must forgive the past. Forgiveness will help all Americans to flourish. Unforgiveness only creates problems because the victims cannot move forward. Hatred among any Americans will only bring about fear, separation and continued prejudice, which are not in God's will. Thank God for someone that is not afraid to tell the truth, from his perspective.

Janice –Corbett- Lovelady
Teacher Montevallo Elementary School
Montevallo, Alabama

TABLE OF CONTENTS

Preface

The United States government created a national pledge that was to be learned and repeated by each child in every grade school in America. It was this way in 1964 when I attended Almont Elementary School, and it should be so today.

Pledging allegiance shows responsibility, which is a character trait that every person ought to possess. Character is shaped during childhood. Responsibility is learned during childhood. The American government, therefore, was wise for instituting the practice of saluting "Old Glory," for it fosters a sense of responsibility in children and plants the seeds of loyalty and devoted support of this country in their hearts. Some of them will honor that oath by defending it with their lives. Some will dedicate their lives to developing, maintaining, and preserving its governing bodies. Some will choose to fortify this country's place as a leader in the technology, literary, and medical fields. Most of them will be good citizens, obeying the laws of the land, paying their taxes, voting, and executing righteousness. If all of this emanates from a two-sentence verse, then it is a good thing.

Pledging allegiance is a good thing for all Americans. We are a people of many ethnic groups, but we are united under one nationality. We are Americans. We are one nation under God, with a common goal to be under one noble flag: the Red, White, and Blue.

This book speaks to all Americans in one way or another. As adult Americans we set the examples for our children, whether good or bad. They will follow our lead. This is our country, and no one will care for it, protect it, and love it like Americans. If we Americans do not push forward to making ourselves better through forgiving the past, then we will eventually poison the minds of the children and turn them against this country. Our values will become the values of human philosophy; we know from philosophers that human philosophy has never been stable. Our values are those of the Holy Bible. These very values keep us from destroying ourselves.

Our legacy is greater than what we realize. Great events in our history correlate with Bible prophecy, from the celebration of the resurrection of our Lord (Easter), to the freedom of the slaves (Emancipation Proclamation Act), and the Azusa Street outpouring of the Holy Spirit. These events all spoke of new beginnings. Interestingly, they all happened in the month of April, the same month as the Exodus of the children of Israel from Egypt. God authored all of these colors and events according to His divine providence, as proclaimed in Exodus chapters 12 and 25.

This government is here to stay, our biblical values are here to stay, and each legal ethnic group is here to stay. What binds us all together is the glorious red, white, and blue American flag. This is the issue.

CHAPTER 1
MY COUNTRY, LAND THAT I LOVE

The United States of America, originally known as Columbia, is the greatest country in the world and the sole superpower that seeks the good of all mankind. Her republic is one of the most populous, wealthiest, and progressive countries in the world. The land extends from east to west divided into four parts: (1) the Atlantic Plains extend from the Atlantic Ocean to the Allegheny Mountains; (2) the Mississippi Valley and the Great Central Plains extend from the Allegheny Mountains west to the Rocky Mountains; (3) the Western Highlands; and (4) the Pacific Slopes extend from the Rocky Mountains to the Pacific Ocean. America is located on the North American Continent in the Western Hemisphere. It has been here since the world was created nearly six thousand years ago. It is separated from Europe by the Atlantic Ocean. It is over 3.7 million square miles, and she is the third or fourth most populous country in the world, with over 300 million people.

She has three coastal areas. The Atlantic Coast extends about 12,360 miles, the Gulf Coast extends about 5,750 miles, and the Pacific Coast extends about 3,250 miles. She has fifty self-governed states that are responsible to the federal government. Within its territories there are many small, rocky islands along the coast of Maine, and on the southern New England coast is a group to which belongs Long Island, the largest island off the coast of the United States. Off the southern coast of California is Santa Barbara.

Each of the fifty states has a capitol where the state's legislative representatives convene to initiate, enact, and enforce laws. Every municipality in each state has a local government to carry out the local business. The states and local governments exist to ensure the freedoms and protect the rights of all citizens and residents.

America is the most advanced country in the world. She has on average the tallest and most illustrious buildings in the world. Skyscrapers grace the skylines of most cities with architectural designs that impress and amaze the beholders. Majestic rolling mountains and green valleys take one's breath away. Superhighways and byways traverse the countryside, snake up and around the mountains, and span the rivers to connect cities and towns. Beautiful flowers carpet the fields in every season, but not in every area. Seasonal changes in climate throughout each section of the country help produce food during each season of the year. The earth is plenteous in all natural vegetation and minerals: gold, silver, copper, brass, and many others. Fertile soil yields all types of crops and fruits: cotton, sugarcane, soybeans, corn, wheat, apples, pears, oranges, peaches, and many more. Everything the heart could desire can be found in America: food, clothing, and furniture stores, banks, theaters, and all sorts of sporting entertainments. We can go to church and worship God according to the Holy Scriptures. We can fight for our rights and win. We can play any sort of sport our hearts desire and our abilities allow. There is nothing that America cannot give.

America is a country of destiny. She has prospered and flourished where other noted societies have suffered desolation and great demise. The splendor of some of the world's greatest empires—ancient Rome, Egypt, Turkey, and Greece—has faded, remembered only by earthen treasures and decaying archaeological remains. America, on the other hand, continues to stand strong, one of the world's wealthiest, most powerful nations, the only existing global superpower.

What the reader must understand is that America was born of divine providence and destined for greatness, with a heritage way beyond Europe. America is the offspring of the misplaced tribes of Israel, the promised seed of Abraham. Our history, our legacy, and our prosperity are not the result of wealth or political prowess; rather, they are the spoils of a higher conquest, a part of a divine plan. In this book I will explicate the significance of that divine order with relevance to our identity as a nation today, in hope that readers will begin to appreciate their American heritage and that Americans will begin to walk in the glory of their inheritance. We have a rich history consisting of Europeans, native Indians, black African slaves, and other groups. We are indivisible, which makes us great.

We went from being without house or mansion to having the finest of all edifices. How did we do it? What made us do it? Who did it? We did it by blood, sweat, and tears: Europeans, Indians, indentured servants, and African slaves. Destiny was the primary purpose. We are great because of the banner that represents us: "Old Glory," the stars and stripes that symbolize the United States of America

CHAPTER 2
A People and Great

It is amazing to look at the history of the world and all the countries and cultures that have derived from the many people that migrated into those areas, and to wonder how long it took to develop their civilizations and cultures. For hundreds of years these people wandered in the political and religious wilderness, trying to find an existence out of darkness to greatness. If they formed anything at all, it lasted a seemingly short time only to become a story from history. However successful they may have been, their success lasted only a short time and is now a memory. Their countries are now filled with broken artifacts and decaying coliseums to be admired by tourists who leave with a thought of what could have been if the leaders had made advancements for the future.

When I see third world countries devoid of great advancements after the many years they have been established, it makes me appreciate the country in which I live. It is a wonder how a country that has existed only 228 years has emerged from the rubble of British rule, to become the greatest nation in the world. Was it a divine order, or did great men establish it? It was divinely designed. God established this nation for His own glory. In this book I hope to show that the Bible has hidden in its pages prophecies foretelling America's greatness and wealth. I hope to give enough biblical facts to prove my assertions without exasperating the reader with too many Scriptures to research.

If a nation is born for greatness as a result of divine providence, the events of its history will fortify and strengthen its resolve for the future, even if its leaders turn from God. The belief in the eternal supreme God is the panacea for all weaknesses and imperfections of a nation. America's birth was a promise from God to Abraham. God said to Abraham, "I will make of you great nations." The apostle Paul wrote, "So then those who are of faith are blessed with believing Abraham" (Galatians 3:9) A wise man said, "It is the glory of God to conceal a matter. But the glory of kings is to search out a matter" (Proverbs 25:2). If there are questions, we must answer them through research. Every great, strong, established   government was and is in the plan of God for His divine purpose and plan. America is a great country with its purpose of evangelizing the world. This obvious fact is seen every day by the nations we help. According to Psalm 75:6-7, promotion of nations comes only from God. The Founding Fathers acknowledged God's hands in the birth of this country. America not only has a rich legacy, but also a future that is rich in purpose.

We are the offspring of the misplaced tribes of Israel, in particular Ephraim and Manasseh. Abraham, Isaac, and Jacob were not fictional characters. These men lived in our world many years ago. They worshiped the only God of heaven and earth. To deny that these men actually lived is to deny that we are presently living on this earth. I remember sitting next to a fellow student in one of my philosophy classes. As we were discussing rhetoric and persuasive arguments, he told the class that he did not exist, and we must accept it. I told him that I would pinch him, and he must not retaliate because he did not exist. If I had pinched him, he would have realized that he existed with the other students of the class. Unlike the philosophical babbling of that student, the fact that there is an Israeli nation today proves the validity of the old patriarchs Abraham, Isaac, and Jacob.

In hindsight, Americans feel that they are a part of these great men and women from Israel's history. We read about their history more than any other country in the world. We worship their God and Messiah. We honor their prophets and kings. We sing their songs and pray their prayers. We read, study, and quote from their book more than any other book in the world. Every year their book, the Holy Bible, is the number one best seller in our country. We have taken one of their citizens as our own citizen. He never walked on American soil or mentioned our name, but we celebrate his birthday as if he had a major part in our history. We have given him a holiday that is celebrated with greater respect than people such as George Washington, Abraham Lincoln, or Martin Luther King Jr. Why are we so fascinated with Abraham, Isaac, and Jacob, their culture, and their offspring? Maybe we are a bigger part of them than we think!

The Bible is a book of prophecy foretelling the history of all mankind and future of the people we know as the Jews in the land of Israel. Whether or not one chooses to believe, the Bible prophecies are true. Israel is a nation today because God said it would be, and He had it written in a book. Every great nation is mentioned between its covers. Did God leave out such a prominent country as America? Where are we mentioned? The all-seeing eye of God did not overlook a nation of so great prominence. America is not mentioned by its actual name, but it is mentioned in context by Jacob (Genesis 38:19-20) and by some of the other prophets.

Perception is based on people's understanding and insightful knowledge regarding a thing that affected their emotions. After experiencing America's greatness, Winston Churchill declared before the United States Congress: "He must indeed have a blind soul who cannot see that some great purpose and design is being worked out here below of which we have the honor to be the faithful servants." After the fall of France, he said, "We shall defend our island whatever the cost may be; we shall fight on beaches, landing grounds, in fields, in streets and on the hills. We shall never surrender and even if, which I do not for the moment believe, this island or a large part of it were subjugated and starving, then our empire beyond the seas, armed and guarded by the British Fleet, will carry on the struggle until in God's good time the New World with all its power and might, sets forth to the liberation and rescue of the Old."

Is this prophecy or the words of an intelligent, brave, war genius? I say it is prophecy. From the time we defeated the British, to the time of these profound words of Churchill, America's strength was understood as having come from the God of heaven. We should no longer ignore our divine call, nor should we accept the treasonous attitude of those who wish to take God out of the hearts and minds of those of us who love this country. God called this nation out of Abraham and established us as a great people.

OUT OF ABRAHAM

God promised Abraham, "I will make you a great nation; I will bless you and make your name great; and you shall be a blessing. I will bless those who bless you, and I will curse him who curses you; and in you *all families of the earth* shall be blessed" (Genesis 12:2-3, emphasis added).

The word *blessing* means "to confer increase upon the one to whom favor is given."[1] When someone has been blessed by God, they are the envy of others and many times spoken evil of because of the goodness bestowed on them by the Creator. God promised that if any person or people would bless Abraham, He would in turn bless them. The only way to bless Abraham is through the nation of Israel and the church. God promised to give Abraham a son. Through that seed all the earth would be blessed.

God also promised that He would curse them that curse Abraham. *Cursed* means "to be belittled, stop the progress of, to hinder, and to make void." In a technologically advanced world, most of the people that are fighting against Israel, Great Britain, and America appear to be nomadic. When one asks, why is America so blessed? I will quote what Geno Auriemma said in 2004 when asked why he thought the University of Connecticut would win the girls' basketball championship: "Why are we going to win? We have Diana and they don't." In like manner, why is America so great? We support Israel and they don't.

"As for Me, behold, My covenant is with you, and you shall be a father of *many nations*. No longer shall your name be called Abram, but your name shall be Abraham; for I have made you a father of *many nations*. I will make you exceedingly fruitful; and I will make nations of you, and *kings* shall come from you" (Genesis 17:4-6, emphasis added). The promise to Abraham was that God would bring from his and his wife Sarah's loins many nations; not just the nation of Israel, which consisted of the twelve tribes from Jacob, but also the nations that would come from one or more of Jacob's sons. Considering the fact that Abraham was the father of faith, the nations that would come from him would represent his faith toward the true God of heaven and earth.

God further illustrated His point with regard to this promise: "And the LORD said, 'Shall I hide from Abraham what I am doing, since Abraham shall surely become a great and mighty nation, and all the nations of the earth shall be blessed in him?'" (Genesis 18:17-18). If all the nations would accept the God of Abraham through Jesus Christ, they would not have as much suffering as they do now. But it is in Abraham that a nation is blessed. Accept this revelation or reject it, but if we take a look at the countries that are constantly suffering and check whom or what they worship, it will be quite evident that the Lord is not the center of their worship.

As for the objective and the purpose laid out for Abraham, God was very clear and direct: "But God said to Abraham, 'Do not let it be displeasing in your sight because of the lad or because of your bondwoman. Whatever Sarah has said to you, listen to her voice; for in Isaac your seed shall be called' " (Genesis 21:12). Abraham had other children, including an older son Ishmael, but the promised seed (the Messiah) and blessed nations would come through the loins of Isaac. As of today, all the other descendents of Abraham that came from Hagar and Keturah are far less advanced than the descendents of Isaac. Is God partial or unfair? No! He is God. He does what He wills without apology (Romans 9:22-26).

There is a direct line between Abraham's descendents and the United States, both naturally and spiritually. If we follow the lineage of Judah and Joseph's sons, we will see a mystery unfold right before our eyes. Abraham was the father of Judah's and Joseph's sons. Abraham is the father of those whose faith is in Christ (the church). A careful study of the migration of Joseph's descendents will place them in the British Isles, which eventually birthed the government of America.

Judah Holds the Scepter until the Coming of Christ

Our main focus is on Joseph's sons. They were the ones that gave us our prosperity. Some of the descendents of Judah's sons gave their monotheistic beliefs to some Europeans and black Africans. But, whatever land the Israelites where scattered to, they carried with them the promise of greatness that God made to their fathers Abraham, Isaac, and Jacob. The birthrights would pass through them according to the following birth order that we find in the all the scared writings:

Abraham begot Isaac

Isaac begot Jacob

Jacob begot twelve sons—God spoke to Jacob: "I am God Almighty. Be fruitful and multiply; a nation and a *company of nations* shall proceed from you, and kings shall come from your body" (Genesis 35:11, emphasis added).

The main premise of Bible history is to show God's provision for Israel because of Abraham, through which the Christ would come and be Savior and King of the world. Christ would come to sit upon the throne that was given to David of the tribe of Judah. The prophets and scribes were careful to record the lineage leading up to and after the birth of David. We have already discussed the three patriarchs, so I will begin with the genealogy of Judah.

Jacob's fourth son, Judah, begot twins, Perez and Zerah. Zerah put his hand out of the womb, but Perez was born first, breaching the birthright and kingly order that would have belonged to his brother Zerah. The royal line should have proceeded from the loins of Zerah, but instead it came from Perez (Genesis 38:27-30). This was not the first time that the birthright had been switched. Jacob received his brother Esau's blessing with the help of his mother, Rebekah (Genesis 27:1-41). The lineage of Judah would hold the scepter for the nation of Israel *until* the coming of Christ. The birthright would normally have belonged to Jacob's oldest son Reuben, but God gave it to Joseph through his two sons.

The royal lineage would come through these sons:
Perez begot Hezron
Hezron begot Ram
Ram begot Amminadab
Amminadab begot Nahshon
Nahshon begot Salmon
Salmon begot Boaz
Boaz begot Obed
Obed begot Jesse

God Himself was the king of Israel. After the Exodus when the Israelites settled back in the land of Canaan, God assigned judges that led the people to victory over their enemies. The last judge over Israel was Samuel. Samuel was old, and his sons were in no spiritual condition to judge. So the elders came to Samuel and requested a king like the other nations around them. Samuel felt as though the people had rejected him, but God, the true King of Israel, told him not to feel rejected because it was He (God) they had rejected (I Samuel 8:7).

11

God gave them Saul from the tribe of Benjamin. The person that God truly wanted to put in this ordained office was a man from the tribe of Judah, but he was yet unborn. David, the son of Jesse, would later be anointed king, but he could not take the throne until Saul was dead.

Jesse begot David

David was a man after God's own heart. He was anointed king, and Israel became a great nation. Under him Jerusalem was established as the capital and holy city (Mt. Zion). This throne would be given to David's male descendents forever, until the coming of Christ.

David begot Solomon

Solomon begot Rehoboam

After Solomon's death, the nation was split. The kingdom of Israel was divided among the northern and the southern tribes. It was now called the house of Israel (northern), and the house of Judah (southern). Judah, including the tribe of Benjamin and the Levites, were called the Jews. God took the other ten tribes from Solomon's descendents and gave them to Jeroboam and his descendents. Jeroboam was from the tribe of Ephraim. By choosing one from the tribe of Ephraim, God fulfilled the prophecy giving to Joseph by Jacob that his sons would be kings in another land, and that those lands would be very wealthy. God was training Ephraim for royalty. I believe this to be so because, according to Genesis 49:10, only the tribe of Judah could be the true ruler of Israel. If the tribe of Ephraim was trained for royalty, then it would be natural for that bloodline to continue its royal quest to rule in another land. Therefore, God had to send them to another land to rule. According to the prophet Ezekiel, God would one day make them one nation again through the Christ (Ezekiel 37:15-22). But until then Judah had the scepter. Ephraim could not rule alongside Judah.

"And when Rehoboam came to Jerusalem, he assembled all the house of Judah with the tribe of Benjamin, one hundred and eighty thousand chosen men who were warriors, to fight against the house of Israel, that he might restore the kingdom to Rehoboam the son of Solomon. But the word of God came to Shemaiah the man of God, saying, 'Speak to Rehoboam the son of Solomon, king of Judah, to all the house of Judah and Benjamin, and to the rest of the people, saying, "Thus says the LORD, 'You shall not go up nor fight against your brethren the children of Israel. Let every man to his house, for this thing is from *Me.*' Therefore they obeyed the word of the LORD, and turned back, according to the word of the LORD" (I Kings 12:21-24, emphasis added).

The promise of God was that David should never want for a man to sit upon his throne until the coming of Shiloh (whose right it was to have the throne). This was valid as long as there was a kingdom. God was their king, but they desired an earthly king so He called the earthly throne after the name of David. The throne was Christ's before it was given to David. David's throne was a substitute until an appointed time when God would take the throne back. God called it "the throne of David" to honor David's faithfulness to Him.

God did not have to honor a bloodline to accomplish His work. This is why no human being can reconcile the genealogy of Jesus ending with a male. It ended with a female only. Jesus was not from this world. He was the King of Judah and the Lion of the tribe of Judah. He could be the King and the Lion without being part of David's bloodline, because it was His right to recover that which was originally His from the foundation of the world. God has all power to start and stop a thing before there is a thing.

If every natural law regarding the tradition of man is sacred to man, then man is bound by his own laws to fulfill them. Man's law does not bind God, but God keeps His covenant with man to fulfill His own will. Mary, the mother of Jesus, a virgin, was of the house of Levi. How could the Christ be from the house of David, born of a virgin from the tribe of Levi? Joseph, who married Mary, was not royalty; therefore, his adoption of Jesus could not give him royal status; there were no kings for four hundred years.

Though it sounds complicated, this is actually quite simple. God had ordained in Genesis 3:15 that a woman's seed, without the aid of a man, would have inheritance in the world. Further, He saw fit that a woman should inherit the blessing of her father if she had no husband. This, in fact, paved the way for Christ to inherit the birthright through a woman only. This is illustrated in Numbers 26:33; 27:1-8, 11b:

> Now Zelophehad the son of Hepher had no sons, but daughters, and the names of the daughters of Zelophehad were Mahlah, Noah, Hoglah, Milcah, and Tirzah. . . . Then came the daughters of Zelophehad . . . and they stood before Moses, before Eleazar the priest, and before the leaders and all the congregation, by the doorway of the tabernacle of meeting, saying, "Our father died in the wilderness, but he was not in the company of those who gathered together against the LORD, in company with Korah, but he died in his own sin, and he had no sons. Why should the name of our father be removed from among his family because he had no son? Give us a possession among our father's brothers." So Moses brought their case before the LORD. And the LORD spoke to Moses, saying: "The daughters of Zelophehad speak what is right; you shall surely give them a possession of inheritance among their father's brothers, and cause the inheritance of their father to pass to them. And you shall speak to the children of Israel, saying, "If a man dies and has no son, then you shall cause his inheritance to pass to his daughter. . . . And it shall be to the children of Israel a statute of judgment, just as the LORD commanded Moses.

God would accept a high priest only if he was from the family of Aaron. The Roman government had appointed men from the Levitical family, but not from the house of Aaron. Therefore, when it was time for Christ to come, the only way for Him to enter this world was through Aaron's lineage, and His mother must be a virgin (Isaiah 7:14). Christ came through no one's bloodline. Being the firstborn of Mary, born in the family of Levi, He became a priest after the order of Melchizedek. Now, because he was the King from heaven and from the tribe of Levi, He assumed the throne and the priestly office that were rightfully His in the first place. Act 20:28 states the blood of Jesus was God's blood. Therefore, He was the legitimate high priest and King.

Coniah was the last of the royal seed of David, but he had no children that could inherit the throne. Who then was worthy to sit on the throne of David? There was no man. So, God snatched the kingdom from the bloodline of David. If God could snatch the kingdom from the bloodline, but keep the throne intact while there was no kingdom for a king to rule, then it would be an easy thing for Him to form nations from a people of Israel that migrated to the north and west of the land that was conquered by the Assyrians. There is nothing too hard for God.

The Nations That Received the Promise to Become Prosperous

God promised Abraham through Isaac that he would be the father of many nations and that kings would come from him: nations, not just one nation. How would this come to pass? Jacob, the son of Isaac, had twelve sons. His eleventh son was Joseph. Joseph had two sons, Ephraim and Manasseh, by the daughter of Poti-Pherah, the priest of On (Heliopolis). Jacob took the sons of Joseph between his knees. This was a symbol of birthing and adoption. By this act, Jacob was saying that the two sons of Joseph were actually his sons, and the blessing that was bestowed on them was no less than the blessing of the other sons. Jacob laid his hands on these sons and prophesied that they would become a commonwealth of nations. God had taken the birthright of prosperity from Reuben and given it to Joseph through his two sons. Jacob prophesied and said the younger son would be greater than the older son and a multitude of nations would come out of him. But he said the older son would be great as well (Genesis 48:11-22; 49:8-12).

The ten northern tribes under Jeroboam changed the day of the Sabbath, which was the seventh day of the week, to the first day of the week. When they breached the Sabbath Day covenant, they were considered as Gentiles. According to I Kings 12:28-33, he changed the place of worship (Mt. Ephraim) and the type of worship. He made priests from people that were not Levites. God's people were known as the people of Israel because they worshiped on the Sabbath Day. When the ten tribes stopped this practice, they lost their true identity as Israelites or Hebrews. The misperception regarding the Israelites is that they could be identified by looks. This could not be further from the truth. After the invasion of the Assyrians, the king replanted the land with Gentiles. Most of the house of Israel moved to foreign lands north and west of their captivity.

In Judah's line we find that David and Solomon did not look like so-called Jews. Queen Esther did not look like a Jew. The apostle Paul, a Benjamite, was mistaken for an Egyptian. Jesus, who was called Christ, the first son of Mary (from the tribe of Levi), and who was given the title "King of the Jews" by Herod, could not have looked anything like a male descendent of David. The only person he could have looked like would have been his mother and her relatives. His biological father was not from this earth. So, with this said, it would be easy for some of the misplaced Israelites to blend among the Gentile nations and never be recognized as Hebrews. Keep in mind that only the tribes of Judah and Benjamin with the Levites were called Jews.

How could God get Gentile kings from the misplaced Israelites? The answer becomes very clear when we understand that Ephraim and Manasseh were part Israelite and part Gentile. They were linked together in royalty and prosperity. When they left the land of Palestine, they were already considered Gentiles;

the only thing God needed to do was to have them possess foreign land and become the proprietors of it. After they migrated and adapted to the culture, they became the rulers of their land. Their land became great empires, and their offspring became royal seed. Unlike their brother Judah, they were not bound to a certain geographical location; they spread north and west. The Bible called it "planting." They were being planted by the Lord God Almighty in another land to become kings and prosperous.

Part of these tribes migrated into Western Europe—the British Isles. In Hebrew *British* means "covenant man." This would be a perfect name for one that had a covenant. The scattered Israelites also migrated to Germany, France, Belgium, Scandinavia, and into other parts of Western Europe. (After AD 70, some of the Jews migrated to the coast of Northern and Southern Africa).

The prophecy concerning Joseph (Ephraim and Manasseh) contains two signs that should be of interest to us all: the *bullock* and the *horns of the unicorns*. "His glory is like a firstborn bull, and his horns like the horns of the wild ox; together with them he shall push the peoples to the ends of the earth; they are the ten thousands of Ephraim, and they are the thousands of Manasseh" (Deuteronomy 33:17).

According to the chart entitled "The Illustrious Lineage of the Royal House of Britain" (1902), the ancient British Isles are from the lineage of Israel.[2] We know that America was birthed out of Great Britain; therefore, the spirit of America is from the royal seed of Israel that holds the only one true God as the Creator of heaven and earth. The chart gives names of the royal seed from the lineage of Perez and Zerah to King George VI and Queen Elizabeth II. It would be worth any American's time to study and have this chart in his or her possession. Whether we agree or disagree with the premises and the conclusions of this chart, we cannot deny the fact that history agrees with some of the findings in it.

Our Seals and Symbols Represent Our Relationship with Israel

For the purpose of this book, it is not necessary to list all the proofs that relate to America's existence from Abraham to the signing of the Declaration of Independence. It is my unshakable belief through divine perception that America is the sister of Israel. The blessings of Abraham were recognized by our Founding Fathers, and they uttered words that could only been given to them by the Holy Spirit.

On April 30, 1863, Abraham Lincoln, the sixteenth president of the United States, made a profound speech that gave glory to God and fear to the righteous:

"We have been recipients of the choicest bounties of heaven. We have been preserved, the many years, in peace and prosperity. We have grown in numbers, wealth and power, as no other nation has ever grown. But we have forgotten God. We have forgotten the gracious hand which preserved us in peace and multiplied and enriched and strengthened us; and we have vainly imagined, in the deceitfulness of our hearts that all these blessings were produced by some superior wisdom and virtue of our own.

Intoxicated with unbroken success, we have become too self-sufficient to feel the necessity of redeeming and preserving grace, too proud to pray to God that made us! It behooves us, then to humble ourselves before the offended Power, to confess our national sins, and pray for clemency and forgiveness."

Without satellite and electronic medium to compare the economy and the strengths of the other world powers, Abraham Lincoln recognized that America had inherited the birthright of Israel until the second coming of Christ, which at that time will cause all nations to be one people. God has set this government to be a moral leader and a publisher of the good news of Jesus Christ.

Is it any wonder that the man God would use to free the slaves and become the greatest president of our history had the same name as the founding father of our faith? There is no way that this man or his parents could have pulled this off without the providence of God. Many things happen because of our actions and volitions, but only God could orchestrate such a plan as to bring this government into existence. Our first flag, the seal of America, the dollar bill, the meaning of the folding of the flag, and other important emblems and symbols all represent the fact that we are the thirteenth tribe of Israel. Mathematics demonstrates to us that there is no such thing as chance, so this government is not here by chance.

The Great Seal of the United States, obverse side[3]

The seal of America was designed by William Barton, a private citizen, and Charles Thomson, secretary of the Continental Congress. The Continental Congress chose a committee to work out a design for the seal on July 14, 1776. It was not until June 20, 1782, that a design was finally accepted. The face of the seal bears the image of a bald eagle—or American eagle—standing alone, with outstretched wings. This signifies that the United States can do the same. (It is therefore no surprise that our current president did not depend on other nations to join him in the fight against Iraq.) On the breast of the eagle is a shield. At the top of the shield is a solid blue bar, which represents the Congress. There are thirteen vertical stripes for the thirteen original colonies. In the eagle's right claw is an olive branch with the thirteen leaves and thirteen olives. The olive branch is used to symbolize peace. The thirteen arrows in its left claw symbolize protection by war. The eagle is looking toward the olive branch, signifying that the United States wants to live in peace but is ready for war. The design shows, too, that the power of peace and war is held by the Congress. In the eagle's beak is a ribbon that bears the Latin motto *E Pluribus Unum*, "out of many [colonies] one [nation]." Over the eagle's head is the constellation, thirteen stars in a "glory," or sunburst, shining through a cloud. It is a sign that the United States has taken its place among the other nations of the world. This image (face side) is used as the Coat of Arms of the United States, and is commonly used on government documents. The back of the seal only appears on the one dollar bill.

The reverse side of the seal[4]

The back of the seal, bearing the image of an unfinished pyramid with thirteen rows of stones, portrays the Union being watched over by the all-seeing eye of God, which is contained within a triangle. In Roman numerals at the base is the date the union was begun—1776. The motto *Annuit Coeptis* above the pyramid means, "He [God] has favored our undertaking." On a ribbon below the pyramid is the motto *Novus Ordo Seclorum*, "[A] new order of the ages."

The new order of the ages simply means that this country's purpose and mission will be like none of the existing countries. From an anatomical perspective, from her head to her feet, she will look completely different from any of her sisters before her. When she is fully dressed, everyone will seek after her beauty. Unlike all the countries before her, she continues to get younger and stronger.

This is consistent with the revelation of America being born from the spirit of Manasseh, which is the thirteenth tribe of Israel. It is no coincidence that we have the Ten Commandments posted in our government facilities. It is no coincidence that the enemies from within are the same people that hate Israel and would like to have all articles associated with Israel removed from any public and private facilities that remind them of our sisterhood. Even though the monument that had the Ten Commandments carved on it had to be removed from one of Alabama's courthouses, the Ten Commandments live on. The Father of the nation of Israel is God. Based on the many statements of the Founding Fathers of this country, the Father of our nation is the same God. Sisters share the same parent. America shares the same prominence as Israel

In 1732 BC, the Assyrian army invaded Samaria (the house of Israel) and took them captive. Israel was scattered north and west of their homeland. Many of them stayed, but a great portion of them migrated to other lands and became known by other names. Many historians have undertaken the hard task of finding what history calls the Lost Tribes of Israel. Volumes of books have been written to trace the whereabouts of these noble people. Most authors and historians agree that these people migrated into Europe after their dispersion. They have been identified as Celt, Gauls, Gimira, Cimmerians, Kimmeroi Khumri, Picts, Jutes, Iskuza, Scythians, Carthaginians, Sakka, Scuthae, Northmen or Normans, Anglo Saxons, Danes, and Vikings. They planted themselves and also were driven into many parts of Asia Minor, Germany, Northern Italy, Northern Spain, Ireland, France, Belgium, Franks, Denmark, Western Germany and Switzerland.[5]

The Statue of Liberty came from France. Some of the Israelites emigrated to France and became primary citizens. Is it any surprise to us that the spirit of the people of France wanted to congratulate the United States for finally bringing complete freedom into this land by giving them this statue? We must understand by the teaching of history that God has established the end from the beginning. Years, months, weeks, days, minutes, and seconds are pieces of puzzles that come together over time. The mystery of America's birth is being revealed day by day. Do not cast off the truth because of the errors that have been written about our existence with the Jews or the house of Israel. The core of the people of the United States of America concedes that the Founding Fathers established our values and morals from principles of a greater power than human philosophy. From the faith of Abraham to Judaeo-Christianity came our root of morality.

CHAPTER 3
The Birth of This New Nation

The story of Christopher Columbus' voyage is familiar to most of us, but few of us know the details and the significance of that voyage. Columbus was born in Genoa, in modern Italy. He was raised by his father to be a weaver. In 1465 at the age of fourteen, he took his first sea voyage and knew at that moment he wanted to sail the seas. Later he studied navigation in Greece and mapmaking in Portugal. During this time he sailed to Africa, Ireland, England, and Iceland. In 1479 he married Felipa Perestrello y Moniz and had a son named Diego. His wife died in 1480, and he never remarried.

In 1453 Constantinople fell to the Moslems, cutting off Europe's eastward trade routes to the Orient and making the finding of a westward route almost impossible. Columbus believed that he had discovered an alternate route, but needed help from an investor such as a government to prove his theory. In 1481 he presented his plans to Portugal, England, France, and Spain. Only Spain accepted his proposal, but it took him six years to convince them to underwrite the plan.

In 1492 King Ferdinand and Queen Isabella of Spain gave Columbus permission to sail to India. After he had convinced some ninety men that the new route to India was just beyond the horizon of the great sea, he was given three ships named the *Nina*, the *Pinta,* and the *Santa Maria.* He set sail on August 3, 1492. After a harsh experience of nearly two months at sea, on October 12, 1492, at 2:00 AM from the *Pinta,* one of his crewmembers (Rodrigo) yelled, "Land! Land!" Columbus had set out for India but stumbled on the Bahamas and Cuba. He had discovered the New World. After landing and stepping off the ship, he found this place already inhabited with civilized, intelligent human beings. According to Howard Zinn, Columbus and his crewmembers treated these people he called Indians very harshly. Already we can see where this road is taking us. But, there is no need to fear; God will show up.

During the first voyage, Las Casas, one of Columbus' crewmembers, described the Indians as friendly, gentle, hospitable, hardworking, and easily entreated. He stated that many of the Indians were killed in the name of digging for gold and treasure. Many of them were killed just to prove a point. On December 25, 1492, the *Santa Maria* ran aground, broke in pieces, and had to be abandoned. Columbus built a fort, where he left some of his men to continue the quest for gold and treasure, and headed back to Spain with the two remaining ships.

On his second voyage Columbus, accompanied by seventeen ships, set sail in October of 1493. He arrived in the Americas (Hispaniola) on November 22, 1493. There he found the men he had left behind dead, possibly killed as a result of the way they had treated the Indians. Columbus, in the name of God, continued to mistreat the Indians against the order of the Monarchs. He repeatedly suggested that slavery was the way to profit from the new colonies. The Monarchs held to their view that it was best to cultivate the natives as friends and make them Christians. Columbus then sailed from Haiti back to Spain.

On his third voyage Columbus left Sanlucar, Spain, on May 30, 1498, accompanied by six ships. He was forced to transport convicts as colonists. He returned to Hispaniola on August 19. Because of his now prestigious status, he viewed himself as one to be feared. He hanged some of his crew for disobeying him. He continued to treat the natives as slaves. Conditions in the colony worsened, and the king and queen sent the Royal Administrator Fracisco de Bobadilla to detain Columbus. Upon Bobadilla's arrival on August 23, 1500, he detained Columbus and his brother Bartolomeo. He arrested them and sent them back to Spain in chains.

After Columbus and his brother were released, he made a fourth and final voyage. His last voyage was his most difficult and challenging of all. He ran into many storms on the ocean. Even while at port his ships sustained heavy damages. He became destitute and would have starved if the Indians had not believed his prediction of a lunar eclipse. He and his crew members went back to Spain, sick and disappointed, where he died some years later on May 20, 1506, still not realizing that he had discovered a New World.[6]

The race to discover a new route to India was lost by Columbus to a Portuguese man named Vasco da Gama. He sailed east around Africa and landed in India on May 20, 1498, and returned from India to Portugal in September of 1499. This was a great event, but it was overshadowed by the discovery and events of the New World.

By the time the New World was being discovered, Europe was heading into the Renaissance Period or the Enlightenment. During this time the Bible was printed for public reading. Martin Luther challenged Catholicism with the knowledge he had of the grace of God. The common people sought public education. The wind of change was blowing from heaven. If God is in control of all things, then we must see His hands in the changes. However, His hands were not in all the cruelty perpetrated by man.

God of creation (Jesus Christ) was shaping and forming the future for world evangelism. First, He must call a people that would glorify His name. Second, He must have a church that would not put man on a pedestal. Last, He must have a country where the government would allow freedom to worship Him in spirit and in truth.

El Almirante Christoval Colon Descubre la Isla Española, y haze poner una Cruz. etc.

Columbus discovering America[7]

*Christopher Columbus. (Bust). Engraving
by Henri Lafort, (1891).*[8]

CHAPTER 4
A PEOPLE CALLED BY HIS NAME

God is our Creator. He loves us and will provide for us if we obey Him. Not all people will obey Him; therefore, He has established a spiritual government called the church. The church is called by His name. Its primary purpose is to evangelize the world with the gospel of Jesus Christ. The message is the love of God to the entire world, and those that take this message will be a people called by His name. The Lord Jesus Christ said to the apostle Peter, "On this rock I will build My church, and the gates of Hades shall not prevail against it" (Matthew 16:18). John 1:12 states, "But as many as received him, to them He gave the right to become children of God . . ."

For the purpose of this book, the word we will use for *church* is *ecclesia* (Greek *ekklesia*).   It represents a body of people that is called out by God through faith in the blood of the Lord Jesus Christ. Individually and collectively, people join this church initially without any duties or obligation to man. The work of redemption is accomplished solely by the Spirit of Christ within the spirit of man. All allegiance is given to God, and as a result men become faithful and dedicated to His church. Any attempts to form a church in God's name outside of the doctrine of the apostles would be a rejected church.

In AD 30 the New Testament ecclesia started when the Lord poured out His Spirit on the 120 plus persons in an upper room in Jerusalem on the day of a Jewish feast celebrated in June, according to our calendar. This feast day was called the Day of Pentecost. This was a day of rejoicing and spiritual renewal. Those who received the Spirit became the first to enter the ecclesia and boldly proclaimed the name of the Lord in every city and province. The power they received from God enabled them to cast out devils, heal the sick, and raise the dead. They showed the same love of God that Jesus had manifested. The ecclesia affected the entire known world directly and indirectly. From AD 30 to AD 325, the ecclesia went through severe persecution continually.

During the first century, with the aide of the apostles, Christianity grew rapidly through Asia Minor, Greece, Italy, and possibly the Far West. Christianity was a new religion with a totally different concept. Because of its message of grace and salvation by the blood of Jesus Christ, many elitists and those of great authority rejected it. Heathen practices were being abolished, but Christians were being killed because of the name of Jesus Christ. The more Christians that were martyred, the faster other people would come to the Lord for salvation from sin.

Christianity was a *religio illicita* (illegal religion). It was the policy of the Roman Empire to tolerate the religions of conquered peoples only as long as they did not attempt to proselytize. Judaism was a *religio licita* (legal). The Greeks and Romans with their pagan gods and customs and the Jews with their monotheistic beliefs and customs were accepted religions because they did not proselytize. The essential proselytizing spirit of Christianity outlawed it, along with it being reckoned among secret societies or *collegia* that were contrary to the law.

Christianity was considered an outcast religion, its teaching too stratospheric for the mainstream to touch. The influential classes hated Christianity. Christians' refusal to participate in idolatrous rites and to frequent the pagan temples, and the exclusion from their homes, and of necessity, their persons of all symbols of idolatry, led them to be looked upon as atheists and enemies of the gods.[9]

From AD 98 to AD 313 Christianity was a rejected religion. In AD 313, Emperor Constantine ordered that Christians no longer be persecuted. After AD 313, Rome created the Catholic Church and established a pontiff as the head of it. He would be called the Pope. A papal order declared that there was only one church and one religion. That church would be called the Holy Roman Catholic Church or Universal Church. The papal order decreed that all who would not obey would be killed. The government and the church became one. The authority of the apostolic message was challenged, changed, diluted, polluted, and mutilated. Pagan men adopted and accepted the Christian theology, but not the God of the Christians.

In AD 313 the Edict of Milan gave Christianity a place with the rest of the religions, and paganism was outlawed. However, that did not stop some from their pursuit of mixing both religions. The Roman Church did not preach Christ; it preached Catholicism, which was a mixture of paganism, worship of man, and governmental control over the souls of men. But God instructed His ecclesia to teach the love of Christ, holiness, and the forgiveness of sins. To teach otherwise would be an indication that that ecclesia was not God's. This period in AD 313 was the beginning of the Dark Ages. God in His own time would establish a nation that would foster the spirit of the twelve tribes of Israel in a nation that would propagate the gospel and let men and women freely choose to accept or reject His way of salvation. The spirits of the tribes of Zebulun and Naphtali are the tribes that represent evangelism, support, and funding for it. (See Genesis 49:13, 21; Matthew 4:12-17.) These spirits would be revived in God's own time. The spirits of these tribes would freely give funds to missionary work and take the gospel to the world. Then men, women, and children would be filled with His Spirit to do His work again at an appointed time. The Roman Catholic Church went to the entire known world and forced its brand of Christian religion on all that were under her control. This was not the way God intended for people to believe in Him.

From AD 325 to AD 451 four different councils were held to settle disputes regarding church theology, including such subjects as the Godhead to the method of salvation:

AD 325 The Council of Nicaea—the deity of Christ as the Son of God
AD 384 The Council of Chalcedon—the deity of The Holy Spirit
AD 431 The Council of Ephesus—human beings as totally depraved
AD 451 The Council of Chalcedon—Christ is both man and God

In the 1980s, Dr. Gene Scott of California made a simple but profound statement regarding the teaching of these councils. He said, "God is one, and His Church is one with many members. God stands alone without any help from anyone or anything. God doesn't need us to determine who he is. He manifests himself any way he chooses." The original apostles had no problems understanding who Jesus was. They had council meetings in Jerusalem to discuss the law and grace issues, but that was cleared up before the end of the first century.

During the Dark Ages, the Holy Spirit's manifestation of power was replaced with human intellect and world government. Even though it appeared on the surface that persecution had stopped, the Catholic Church created another form of persecution that was called the Inquisition. The Inquisition used a form of torture that made true Christians and landowners confess to treason, heresy, and witchcraft. The practice humbled business owners, landowners, and men of political power until they submitted all of their assets to the church. The church forbade the reading of Scriptures. They killed John Knox because he translated the Bible for all to read. For hundreds of years the gates of hell assaulted the true believers, but evil could not prevail, just as it could not prevail during the four hundred years of Israel's bondage in Egypt. Israel is the natural church, and the believers in Jesus Christ are the spiritual ecclesia.

A Church That Would Not
Put Man on a Pedestal

Jesus Christ is the only head of God's ecclesia. Jesus told the disciples not to be called father or call any man father, because there was only one Father and He was in heaven (Matthew 23:6-12). Rome had given the popes "all power." They were called the Vicars of Christ, and as such they were considered infallible. If people had been allowed to read the Bible they would have known that all men were fallible, and that God alone was perfect in holiness and judgment. For hundred of years these popes brought shame to the church, the world, and themselves. Whenever man is enthroned as God, and then accepts that position, God will bring him down to the ground (Ezekiel 28:11-19).

At the time Columbus was discovering the New World, the Vatican elected Pope Alexander VI (1492-1503). His birth name was Roderigo Borgia. He had been a cardinal for thirty-six years and was sixty when he became pope. Besides fathering a number of children of whose mother(s) nothing was known, he had a family of four children by a Roman woman with whom he lived. He allegedly was capable of any crime that furthered his interests or the interests of his children.[10] Such was the character of the popes before and after Alexander. Many of these men violated their church's oath of celibacy, and principally violated the law of God that stated men should marry. The purpose of this book does not allow me the time to tell of all the murderous schemes that went on in the papal offices. The contradiction in morals and the inhibition of religious freedom was drowning the people as they saw in the spirit a light shining in another country.

At this time God was speaking to a man named Martin Luther. Luther was born in Eislesben, Germany, on November 10, 1483, during the time of the Renaissance. At age twenty-two he received his master's degree from the University of Erfurt, Germany. Two years later he received his first doctor's degree in theology. At the tender age of twenty-six he was a theology teacher in the monastery.

Luther became a very important figure and was invited to Rome where he associated with dignitaries of all levels. After seeing the immoral practices of Rome and the same practices from his superiors, he went back to Wittenberg. While thinking of his many trips and debates, he became spiritually and mentally disturbed over what he had seen. Exhausted, frustrated, angry, and not knowing where to turn, he went to his study. In 1512 while pouring over the pages of the Bible in his monk's cell with his Bible open to Romans 1:17, he read, "*The just shall live by faith.*"[11] This was his gateway to Paradise.

On All Saints Day (Halloween) 1517, Martin Luther nailed his "95 Theses" to the Castle Church door. The "95 Theses" were propositions against the teaching of the Roman Church in respect to the indulgences, morality, leadership, and other teachings he felt were not according to the Word of God. Unlike all the other postings that were placed on the door, this one caught the people's attention and caused much commotion for many years. Because of the immoral papacy and the practices of church's rituals, Luther was determined to show the hierarchy of the church that God was the head of the ecclesia, and His grace was the only means of salvation.

Luther did not have the backing of the government because the church ruled the government, and government ruled the church. One man or a small group of people could not effect change. There had to be a country to join in the fight to break away from papal power in order for true change to persist. Henry VIII persuaded Parliament to pass a series of acts between 1529 and 1536 to take away the Pope's authority in England. This was accomplished; however, the church returned to the Roman Catholic Church in 1553. When Elizabeth I took the throne, the House of Commons pressured her to renounce the pope, which she did in 1559. The Church of England has been Protestant ever since.[12] The split from Rome allowed the growth of Christian thought but not true autonomy. This breakaway would be of great importance for the New World. King James I took the throne in 1603. From 1603-1611, he had the Bible translated for public reading. After this Authorized Version became public, the people sought God for themselves. When they were withstood, America became even more enticing. So they took this new Book and headed to the Promised Land.

A COUNTRY WHERE THE GOVERNMENT WILL ALLOW RELIGIOUS FREEDOM

Belief is one thing, but understanding what we believe is another. We must have the right to exercise the free will of thought without the fear of being beheaded. From the time the New World was discovered, until the time of the Reformation of the 1500s, true Christians were not allowed to think differently from the established religious system. In order for missionaries to be true missionaries, God had to establish a government that would not force its citizens to be of one religious understanding, regardless of the eternal consequences. While the wind of change was blowing from heaven throughout Europe, God was preparing the New World for a task greater than what anyone could have ever dreamed. All the simultaneous changes in all the aforementioned countries were birth pains to deliver the baby that would be named *America*.

God had to move Christianity from the hands of Rome and Europe to allow its true spiritual nature to rule. It was never God's intent that the ecclesia would be a religion for males only. It was birthed by the Spirit and has to be operated by born-again spirits of both males and females with God in control. This could only happen in a new land with a new government at a time of God's own choosing.

CHAPTER 5
FREE LAND?

After Columbus's first voyage, and his return to Spain with the good news about the land of gold and other precious materials, the news spread like wildfire. Soon there were expeditions from the north, east, south, and west, trying to "cash in" on the Promised Land. Below is a list of men that came to the New World with expectations of obtaining the bountiful blessings that the New World had to offer.

1499—Amerigo Vespucci wrote a letter to a friend claiming to have discovered a part of the South American coast. An account of this voyage was published. The German geographer Waldseemuller, who had read the account, named the new continent after him—America.

1500—Cortereal, a Portuguese man, explored the coast from Labrador to Nova Scotia.

1512—Ponce De Leon, seeking a legendary fountain of youth, discovered Florida.

1539—Coronado, along with a force of Spaniards, marched northward from Mexico to Colorado and Kansas, and discovered the Grand Canyon of the Colorado River. De Soto, at the same time, led an army of about a thousand into northwest Florida. He reached the Mississippi in 1541.

1582—Spanish monks planted missions in New Mexico and Arizona.

1584—Sir Walter Raleigh sent out an expedition under Captain Arthur Barlow. The explorers landed at Pamlico Sound and named the region Virginia in honor of Elizabeth.

1587—Raleigh dispatched another expedition, consisting of two ships with 150 men and women, to Roanoke Island. John White was the Governor. Virginia Dare, the first white child born in America, was born here.

LAND IS NOT FREE

Colony Name	Year Founded	Founded By
Virginia	1607	London Company
Massachusetts	1620	Puritans
Maryland	1634	Lord Baltimore
Connecticut	1635	Thomas Hooker
Rhode Island	1636	Roger Williams
Delaware	1638	Peter Minuit and New Sweden Company
New Hampshire	1638	John Wheelwright
North Carolina	1653	Virginians
South Carolina	1663	Eight Nobles with a Royal Charter from Charles II
New Jersey	1664	Lord Berkeley and Sir George Carteret
New York	1664	Duke of York
Pennsylvania	1682	William Penn
Georgia	1732	James Edward Oglethorpe

From 1607-1689, the explorers began claiming portions of the New World for their countries. Colonies were set up and named. The Southern Colonies were Virginia, Maryland, and the Carolinas; The New England Colonies were Massachusetts, New Hampshire, Connecticut, and Rhode Island; the Middle Colonies were New York, New Jersey, and Delaware. As time went on others were added, but we are only interested in the original thirteen for our main point.

English settlers were growing and establishing colonies. From 1607-1733, the English established thirteen prosperous colonies. By 1750 nearly 2 million men, women, and children were living there. During the 150 years of colonial history, most of those who settled in America came from the British Isles. (Keep in mind that the displaced Israelites were founders of the British Isles.) They came from England, Scotland, Ireland, and Wales. Many came from other countries in Europe. Still others came from Africa. Most of the Africans were transported to the New World as slaves.[13]

Why would people risk coming across the ocean to live in the New World? The economy in England was terrible. People needed jobs and opportunities to start a new life. Many believed that religion was a matter of choice, and they wanted the right to worship God without governmental restriction. Rich business owners would stand to gain a lot of money through property. America was the land of opportunity. The idea of freedom appealed as well. They asked, why not risk it?

Captain John Smith led the expedition to establish territories south of New York and the Carolinas. In December of 1606, the *Goodspeed*, the *Susan Constant*, and the *Discovery*, filled with money and people, sailed from England to colonize the New World. They landed in Virginia in April of 1607. With the arrival of these ships, the Spanish government hoped to start Spanish colonies.

Many of the settlers that came to the New World died because they did not want to work or because they did not know how to coax a crop from uncultivated land. Many of these people who perished were only interested in finding the gold they had heard about. But salvation was in the hands of strong and caring leaders like John Smith. He caused the colony to prosper and thereby helped to save many lives. He made friends with the Indians. They taught him and the others how to live off this strange land.

The financial backers of the Virginia Company of London that had invested in the expedition of the three ships commanded by John Smith had lost a great deal in the New World. The colonists were not producing as expected, mainly because they did not own the houses or the land. When they saw their investment dissipating, the owners had to develop another strategy. By giving a portion of land to the settlers, they felt the settlers would be more responsible in maintaining it. Not only that, but if the men had wives and families they would care even more. This proved to be the right move. Things began to prosper. However, the task of maintaining the level of prosperity was too great; paying wages was losing too much money.

The settlers tried to force the Indians into slavery. By enslaving the Indians they could get free labor, thereby keeping all the money for the owners. The Indians soon fought back. So the owners had to think of another source of free labor. What about indentured servitude? Indentured servants were people who "sold" themselves for a set period of time so they could get ahead later. However, this strategy did not work because these were fellow countrymen and the investors were still losing money. The indentured servants could not be forced to work without being paid, even when the pay was low. They were white English men and women. In order to boost the economy they needed slaves, people that worked without pay. Where could they find such people if the Indians and the indentured servants would not cooperate with the program?

THE COST OF FREEDOM

Whenever God brings something into existence, He has already worked out the details. Remember that after Jerusalem was destroyed in AD 70 and the Jews were dispersed through the world, some went to the coast of Africa, taking their monotheistic theology with them. About 1440, Antam Goncalvez, a Portuguese sea captain, captured three Moors somewhere along the Atlantic coast of Africa. In 1442 these Moors regained their freedom by handing over in exchange ten black Africans, who were taken to the Portuguese city of Lisbon and sold into slavery. On a second trip Goncalvez brought back more Blacks. Before 1460, nearly one thousand Blacks a year were being taken to Portugal. The slaves were taught about Christianity, and most became Christians. By the end of the century the Portuguese were supplying slaves to Spain.

The following article proves that black African Christians were taken into slavery at the beginning of America's history, even though this group of black Africans came over after the slave trade ended.

Key West Florida, May 20, 1860—On the morning of the 30th of April last, the United States steamer Mohawk, Lieutenant Craven commanding, came to anchor in the harbor of this place, having in tow a bark of the burden of about three hundred and thirty tons, supposed to be the bark *Wildfire*, lately owned in the city of New York. The bark had on board five hundred and ten native Africans, taken on board in the River Congo, on the west side of the continent of Africa. She had been captured a few days previously by Lieutenant Carven within sight of the northern coast of Cuba, as an American vessel employed in violating our laws against the slave-trade. She had left the Congo River thirty-six days before her capture.

Soon after the bark was anchored we repaired on board, and on passing over the side saw, on the deck vessel, about four hundred and fifty native Africans, in a state of entire nudity, in a sitting, or squatting posture, the most of them having their knees elevated so as to form a resting place for their heads and arms. They sat very close together, mostly on either side of the vessel, forward and aft, leaving a narrow open space along the line of the centre for the crew of the vessel to pass to and fro. About fifty of them were full-grown young men, and about four hundred were boys aged from ten to sixteen years. It is said by persons acquainted with the slave-trade and who saw them, that they were generally in a very good condition of health and flesh, as compared with other similar cargoes, owing to the fact they had not been so much crowded together on board as is common in slave voyages, and had been better fed than usual. [Note: It is a fact that the majority of people who have faith in God are able to handle difficult circumstances better than the ones without faith.]

We saw on board about six or seven boys and men greatly emaciated, and diseased past recovery, and about a hundred that showed decided evidences of suffering, from inanition, exhaustion, and disease. Dysentery was the principal disease. But notwithstanding, their sufferings, we could not be otherwise than interested and amused at their strange looks, motions, and actions. The well ones looked happy and contented, and were ready at any moment to join in a song or a dance whenever they were directed to do so by "Jack"—a little fellow as black as ebony, about twelve years old, having, a handsome and expressive face, an intelligent look, and a sparkling eye. The sailors on the voyage had dressed "Jack" in a sailor costume, and had made him a great pet. When we were on board "Jack" carried about in his hand a short cord, not only as the emblem but also as the instrument of his brief delegated authority. He would make the men and boys stand up, sit down, sing, or dance just as he directed. When they sang, "Jack" moved around among them as light as a cat, and beat the time by slapping his hands together, and if any refused to sing, or sang out of time, Jack's cord descended on their backs. Their singing was monotonous. The words we did not understand. We have rarely seen a more happy and merry-looking fellow than "Jack."

[Note: How can a person in the chains of slavery be so full of joy? Can there be a reason to sing songs and rejoice if you are in the pit of despair? Hatred is the only expressed emotions for forced slavery. Jack's disposition can only be explained by one's understanding that his soul was enlightened by a power of joy greater than the human emotions.]

About sundown they all lay down for the night upon a camp-bed, and were covered over with blankets. And now a scene took place which interested us very much, but which we did not understand and can not explain. The woman standing up slapped her hands together once or twice, and as soon as all were silent she commenced a sort of recitation, song, or prayer in tone and manner much like a chanting of the Litany in Catholic churches, and every few moments the voices of then or fifteen others were heard in the some tone, as if responding. This exercise continued about a minute. Now what could this be? It looked and sounded to us very much like Christians chanting together an evening prayer on retiring to rest. And yet we feel quite assured that none of these persons had ever heard of Christ, or had learned Christian practices, or possessed much, if any knowledge of God as a Creator or Preserver of the world. We suspect that it was not understood by them as a religious exercise at all, but as something which they had been trained to go through at the barracoons in Africa or on board the ship.

We visited them in the afternoon, and have done so several times since; and we confess that we have been struck, as many others have been, with the expression of intelligence displayed in their faces, and the beauty of their physical conformation, and the beauty of their teeth. We have been accustomed to think that the civilized negroes of our own country were superior, in point of intelligence and physical development, to the native Africans; but judging only by the eyes, we think it would be difficult to find, any where in our own country, four hundred finer and handsomer-looking boys and girls than these are. To be sure you often saw the elongated occiput, the protruded jaws, and the receding forehead; but you also often saw a head as round, with features as regular as any European's, except the universal flat noses. Little "Jack" has a head as round as an apple.

A number of these negroes—perhaps twelve or fifteen in all—have been more or less at and about Loando, a Portuguese town on the coast, and have learned to speak a little Portuguese. Through an interpreter we learned from them that some four or five—perhaps more, but probably not many—had been baptized at the Roman Catholic missionary station in Loando. Francisco, a young man, says he was baptized by a Franciscan friar in Loando; that he was a slave in Africa, and does not wish to return there. He says he had rather be a slave to the white man in this country. Salvador, a bright-looking, smart lad, has been baptized. Constantia says she was baptized in Loando. She does not remember her father; she was stolen away when she was young, and was sold by her brother. Antoria and Amelia are both fine-looking young women, aged about twenty, and were both baptized at Loando. Madia, a pagan, unbaptized, aged about twenty, has obtained among the white people here who have visited the quarters the name of "The Princess," on account of her fine personal appearance and the deference that seemed to be paid to her by some of her companions. The persons we have here mentioned, including some eight or ten others, evidently do not belong to the same tribe that the rest do. Indeed the whole number is evidently taken from different tribes living in the interior of Africa, but the greater numbers are "Congos." The women we have named have cut or shaved the hair off the back part of their head, from a point on the crown to the back part of either ear. It is the fashion of their tribe. None of the other women are thus shorn. Many of the men, women, boys, and girls have filed their front teeth, some by sharpening them to a point, and others by cutting down the two upper front teeth. The persons above named have their teeth in a natural state.[14]

It is a fact that when people accept Christian principles they act and dress differently. Notice that the writer placed emphasis on some of the "above persons that didn't practice strange behaviors." The writer of the article noticed a difference in many of the detainees, and thought it necessary to describe them as coming from different "tribes." Many Africans were taken from these and other regions of Africa similar to places mentioned in this article. It has to be assumed that people of like faith and practices (as the enslaved Africans on board the *Wildfire*) were taken and brought to this country before the slave trade ended. With the slaves from Spain, these people helped shape the Christian attitude of other slaves. Therefore, Christianity was not introduced to the black African slaves by the white man; they had it before coming here. As a result of the belief they had in God, they became a part of the king's and queen's plans to have a Christian American foundation. From the very foundation of this country, the religious belief was Christ-centered.

Once we understand where many of the black Africans came from, we will be able to understand why they could accept Christianity so easily. From the southern to the northern parts of the coast of Africa, we have discovered that there were many so-called black Jews or black African Jews that were practicing the law of Moses. In the 1990s a group of black Africans identified themselves as the descendents of the Jewish family in the Continent of Africa. They dwelled in those parts for many years. After their discovery, much has been written about the black Jews in Africa. They lived in the same area from which slaves were taken and sold. Is it any surprise that the black Africans who were taken to Portugal and Spain believed in only one God? Their monotheistic belief was more theologically sound than the Christians of Europe. Is it conceivable that God's divine will was in action to remove a people that blessed Abraham into a greater place and status? If these so-called Jewish people were able to pray to the true God while being forced into slavery, and years later become a great people rising out of obscurity, then one must conclude God heard their prayers because His plan to move them to this country was greater than any plan they could have conceived.

THE START OF NORTH AMERICAN SLAVERY

The harsh treatment of the Indian slaves eventually prompted Bartolome de Las Casas, Roman Catholic bishop of Chiapas, to approach the new Spanish king, Charles I, with the proposal that each Spanish settler should be permitted to bring over a certain number of black African slaves. In 1517 this ideal was accepted. From this point thousand of slaves were transported into the Caribbean and later to the mainland. Here in the mainland, black slavery prevailed and, with the development of sugarcane plantations, the slave trade reached colossal proportions beginning around the end of the seventeenth century. Thus a measure of mercy conceived for the protection of Indian natives created the origin of one of the cruelest institutions of all times: black plantation slavery in North America.

In 1505 the Spanish governor of the new territory was granted official authority to import black slaves. The first slaves to be brought to the New World arrived in 1505 at the island of Hispaniola (present-day Haiti and Dominican Republic). The first slaves were imported from Portugal, where they had become Christians. The Christian African slaves would play a very important role in the survival of the slaves in the free world. They had a God that would hear them and would bring deliverance. The supply of slaves from Portugal was limited, and the demand was great. Africa contained an endless supply of Blacks. By 1518 the Portuguese were selling Blacks directly from the West Coast of Africa to the Spanish settlers in the New World.

In 1562 Captain John Hawkins sailed to Sierra Leone, on the West Coast of Africa, and captured three hundred Blacks. His method was to use armed force, kidnapping and burning villagers as they tried to escape. He and his successors encouraged tribal wars and bought captives from the victorious tribal chiefs. The men were chained hand and foot. Together with women and children, they were crammed tightly aboard ships. Half of the slaves died before reaching the New World. Before the slave trade ended in the nineteenth century, over 10 million black African slaves had been imported into North and South America.

The slave trade in the New World English settlements (United States of America) began in 1619 when ships carrying several black Africans landed and were sold by a Dutch trader in Jamestown, Virginia. By 1714 the number of slaves had reached approximately 59,000, and by 1754 approximately 263,000 were in the colonies.[15]

DIVINE APPOINTMENT FOR BLACK AFRICANS

It is extremely important to keep in mind that God is in control of the future and its events. Daniel said, "Blessed be the name of God forever and ever, for wisdom and might are His. And He changes the times and the seasons; He removes kings and raises up kings; He gives wisdom to the wise and knowledge to those who have understanding. He reveals deep and secret things; He knows what is in the darkness, and light dwells with Him" (Daniel 2:20-22). Nebuchadnezzar said, "In order that the living may know that the Most High rules in the kingdom of men, [He] gives it [the spirit of interpretation] to whomever He will, and sets over it the lowest of men" (Daniel 4:17b). It is hard to imagine the loving God of creation placing people in a situation where they were humiliated. It is admirable for someone to agree with such findings. If we are not familiar with the omnipotent character of God, we may conclude that only that which starts out good and finishes good is from God. Quite to the contrary, God sometimes allows His beloved ones to go through the bad so they can gain His goodness. (See Jeremiah 19:2-6.) The means by which He does these things do not, according to human calculations, add up to the end.

We read the Bible and rejoice at the fact that God brought the children of Israel out of Egypt after they had served the pharaohs four hundred years. What we do not usually mention is that God sent them there in the first place! "Then He said to Abram: 'Know certainly that your descendants will be strangers in a land that is not theirs, and will serve them, and they will afflict them four hundred years. And also the nation whom they serve I will judge; afterward they shall come out with great possessions' " (Genesis 15:13-14). God took them in and brought them out. The reason we preach and teach about this wonderful story with such enthusiasm is that it was someone else's history. If it had been *our* history, we would have a problem with it. But, we Americans (both black and white) have a divine history.

I am going out on a limb, but it is a strong one—the limb of truth. Truth can be fought against but never defeated. It is difficult to accept the fact that black Africans were brought as slaves to this country according to the plan of the Almighty. It is also inconceivable that the Almighty did not have the power to prevent these people from being enslaved. If God was the author of the government of the New World, then He also was the author of gathering those that made up her early growth. I do apologized for revealing this profound truth to the Blacks, but I will not apologize for the truth. Some things are better left unsaid because of the damage they will cause. So I must use the Holy

Bible as a shield for revealing information that brings to light a people's struggles. The Bible reveals the weakness and strength of all humans, including our Lord and Savior Jesus Christ. I find in it the strength to reveal this information even while knowing that people sometimes get very upset when truth is revealed. But this historical fact must be revealed because God is the author; I am just the herald that is making it known.

Christian black Africans came to this country before the other Africans arrived so they would be able to help them deal with the pain of slavery. God knew what would happen and made a way for a people to become prosperous; this prosperity could not have come about if it were not for their arrival in this country. "It was the will of God Almighty that Black Africans come to this country."[16] There were and are black Africans that were children of Abraham. A person can be the child of Abraham both biologically and through belief. God was bound to keep His promise to Abraham's children. The promise could only come through the Messiah (Christ). Those who looked for the Messiah were guaranteed prosperous blessings, regardless of how they obtained the promise. It is a great possibility that God took from that believing stock of Africans and sent them to America to fulfill His promise to Abraham. Many of us that are descendents of the black African slaves are from the loins of Abraham through Keturah and some of us through belief in the Messiah. God has kept His promise. This is why we are so successful.

Can anyone deny that the story in Genesis regarding Joseph's enslavement was bad? No, because it *was* bad. He never deserved ill treatment; it was God's plan for him to deliver his own people. Do you think that Joseph could have traveled to Egypt and said, "Mr. Pharaoh, sir, I had a dream that I would deliver my people so I will have to be next in line after you to do it. Give me a portion of your kingdom so that I can have all Egypt report to me." Pharaoh would have said, "Off with his head!" Another dream would have gone down the drain. God put Joseph in that awful slavery condition so that He might get glory out of Joseph's life. Now, because it was God's doing, Joseph saved his family and all of Egypt.

In Daniel 2, King Nebuchadnezzar of Babylon had a dream. He saw an image that represented the earthly kingdoms, both present and future. Each one of these kingdoms came to power as predicted by Daniel. However, the fact that the prophecies came true was not the glory of this story; the glory was that God caused Judah to go through extremely hard conditions so that He might bring Christ at the appointed. Therefore, it is not unforeseeable that God would place a people like the black Africans in a subservient position in the Americas, especially the United States of America, to make them prosperous.

Do you think that the black Africans, now black Americans, would have been allowed to voluntarily come over here with the white Europeans? No way! Understand one thing: the Europeans had all the money and power. Their attitude at that time was that they were the superior race. No one could have penetrated that wall but God. In God's own time a people would be made great along with the Europeans. The following parable says it best.

> There was a man who had four sons. He wanted his sons to learn not to judge things too quickly. So he sent them each on a quest to go and look at a distant pear tree. He sent the first son in the winter, the second in the spring, the third in the summer, and the fourth in the fall.

When they had all gone and come back, he called them together to describe what they had seen.

The first son said the pear tree was ugly, bent, and twisted. The second son said no, it was covered with green buds and full of promise. The third son disagreed; he said it was laden with blossoms that smelled so sweet and looked so beautiful that it was the most graceful thing he had ever seen. The fourth son disagreed with all of them; he said the tree was ripe and drooping with fruit, full of life and fulfillment.

The man then explained to his sons that they were all right because they had each seen only one season in the tree's life. He told them that you cannot judge either a tree or a person by only one season. The essence of who that person is and the pleasure, joy, and love that come from that life can only be measured at the end when all the seasons are up. If you give up when it is winter, you will miss the promise of spring, the beauty of summer, and the fulfillment of fall.[17]

The struggle has been great, but the descendents of the black African slaves have proven that they are a great people. This is why black Americans must pledge allegiance to the country that God has given them so that they may enjoy the prosperity that God has given to America. Like Joseph, we must forgive in order to inherit what is ours. The "means" of getting here may not seem to add up to the "end" of making us part of America's prosperity, but understand this: we would never have what we possess today if we had stayed in the land from which our forefathers were taken. Today black Americans' prosperity far exceeds that of the Blacks in the lands from which they were sold and taken. Europeans meant it for evil, but God meant it for good.

Like the children of Israel who were in bondage in Egypt and who cried unto the Lord of heaven and earth, the black African slaves cried unto the Lord and He heard them and delivered them. He caused them to become citizens of this blessed land. When God delivered them, He also judged those that tried to enslave them. God is still punishing people for their mistreatment of Americans. Companies and individuals that violated the ordinance from God thought they were getting away with crimes committed against these Americans. However, they suffered the punishment they deserved at a later date. Hidden behind the cloud of divine mysteries is God's providential care for those whom He has brought into existence for His purposes. The flag of the United States is a mystery revealed. The flag is a representation of God's handiwork. It protects everyone that is under its waving colors. This is why I pledge allegiance to the flag.

Woody Guthrie wrote the song "This Land Is Your Land." He concluded by stating, "Nobody can stop me . . . this land was made for you and me." Knowing this should make all of America's citizens appreciate, fight for, and pledge their dedication to their land.

Slavery Means More Money in the Bank

Every government that conquered another country or established a new government on new land, needed one thing to jumpstart the economy: slaves. They needed people that would work the fields, pick the fruits, build houses and barns, and produce more slaves—all of this labor for free.

Free labor helps the economy grow much faster than when people have to be paid to do the work. However, America's growth was at the expense of black Africans. After the black African slaves arrived, the economic growth of the colonies soared to great heights.

Without reliving what we already know about the treatment of the African slaves, I will only briefly review the hurtful knowledge of the blood, sweat, and tears that built these colonies before they became a country. The free labor of black African men, women, and children gave this country its start. Without free labor the colonists would not have been able to earn exorbitant profits to put back in the businesses. Without slaves most of them would have gone broke. Just imagine all the fields that needed plowing, all the wood that needed cutting, all the animals that needed tending, and all the food that needed preparing for the bosses and their families and friends. The slaves toiled from sunrise to sunset, with maybe fifteen- to thirty-minute breaks during daylight, if the masters felt it was necessary. The women were not allowed a two-month maternity leave. The mothers and fathers could not teach their children how to do fun games. Just imagine how much money plantation owners saved six days a week, fourteen hours a day, when they did not have to pay for labor.

Because slavery has tainted the American conscience, some writers have tried to make Whites feel less guilty about the enslavement of black Africans by comparing it to indentured servitude. However, these two systems cannot be compared. Slavery is forced upon a person, while indentured servitude is entered into voluntarily. White Europeans who subjected themselves to indenture were never treated as harshly as the black Africans. Without controversy, American slavery was the worst type of slavery that any people should go through. If it were not for what I believe to be divine providence that I should be in this country, I could say that it may have been better if the black Africans were used as human targets or food for the sharks. It would have been a noble thing if all the black slaves had committed suicide. But this would not be so; God's plan was to bring them over the rough and treacherous waters. Many died, but my forefathers made it, and for this I give joyful thanks to God.

In this country the lesson we have learned from Black History is that people's personhood was taken from them. Their whole physique was changed by the brutal working and living conditions they had to endure. Their will was taken. The knowledge that they were made in the image of God was suppressed in them. Their learning ability was taken from them. They were deprived of basic rights as human beings. These people gave everything that human beings could possibly give without any will to say yes or no. On top of that, after sweating in the hot fields or shivering in the cold mines, they were told they did not have a soul. They were bred like animals. When the mothers gave birth, some boss would take the baby after it had been weaned. Adults and children were displayed naked on the auction block as if they were purebred dogs. A former slave, Fountain Hughs stated, "If I thought, had any idea, that I'd ever be a slave again, I'd take a gun and just end it all right away. Because, you're nothing but a dog. You're not a thing but a dog."[18]

The bosses would use the young slave girls for their sexual pleasures. Their mothers and fathers could not say a word except,

"You do what the master tells you to do." The little girls whose innate desire was one day to have the God-given right to fall in love and give themselves to the man of their choice could now never be fulfilled. Slave marriages were not considered legitimate because they were never pronounced husband and wife.[19] What the slave owners never realized was that it was not the public vows that made a marriage; it was the event that happened in the bedchamber. Black slave families never knew what it meant to be a family because at any given time the mother or father could be sold or killed. None of the slave families could look forward to having their families intact in the future. The joy of tomorrow was only for the white families. The slaves could only look forward to more harsh treatment; American slavery was the cruelest form of slavery you could ever imagine.

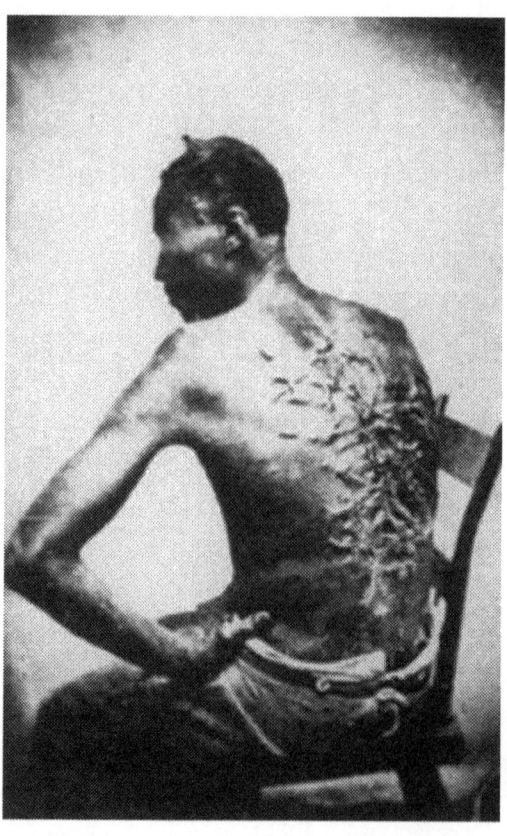

Baton Rouge, La., 2 April, <u>1863</u>: "Overseer Artayou Carrier whipped me. I was two months in bed sore from the whipping. My master come after I was whipped; he discharged the overseer. The very words of poor Peter, taken as he sat for his picture."[20]

Any civilization that has lasted and grown strong did it because of sacrifice. It happened to be the black African slaves whose sacrifice made this country what it is today. The black Africans could have said, "This is our land. We purchased it with our blood and our sons' and daughters' blood." This land was not free. It cost many people their lives. The New World belonged first to the native Indians, second to the black Africans, then the Spanish, English, French, Dutch, and all others. But this is a republic; therefore, it belongs to the United States of America.

The New World was finally colonized. The European governments had pushed the Indians off their own land, but not without the loss of many lives. For the most part, the white man had trained the black Africans to work without pay. Slave owners and the banks that financed them were getting rich and fat. White women were basically in the same class as indentured servants and black African male slaves. They were beaten, refused higher education, and refused upper management jobs. Even though they were white, they had no voice in decision-making. Likewise, they were no better off than the black slave women; they watched their husbands make babies with the slaves and could not do a thing about it. All of this was the brutal truth about the start of the New World. I believe God had His hand in the development of the New World, but not in the cruelty inflicted by the hands of the white Europeans on black Africans, white women, and Indians.

A slave auction at the south. Wood engraving in Harper's
Weekly, **July 13, 1861, Author Theo. R. Davis.**[21]

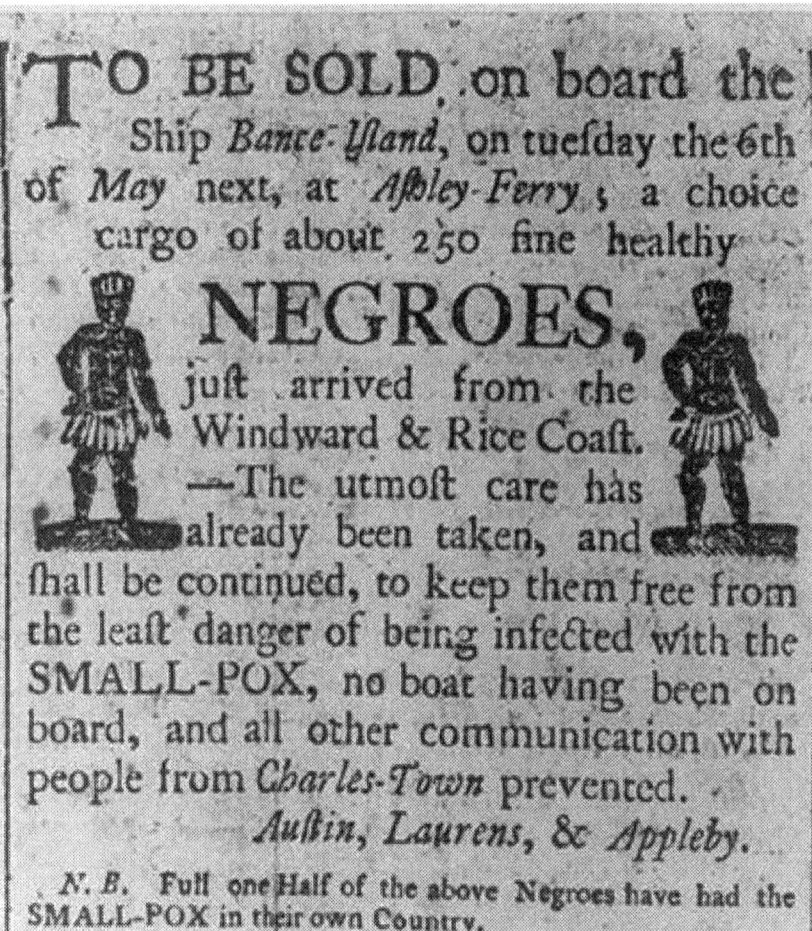

To be sold on board the ship Bance Island[22]

CHAPTER 6
THE MAKING OF A NEW GOVERNMENT

During the time America was forming into a European-like government, other countries were experiencing the pains of old age. From 1562 to 1598 Christianity was pulling away from the dogma of the Roman Catholic Church and the Church of England. There were many religious wars: in France 1568-1648, in Italy 1494-1529, and in Germany 1546-1547.

From the start of the Renaissance and into the middle of the Reformation, a new cry for religious freedom was heard. Prior to the Reformation men had cried for religious freedom but could not get many followers. This time the cry was greater and the people began to follow. The Roman Church and the Church of England heard the cry. Men such as Martin Luther and John Calvin and their followers would not give in to the threat of death. They wanted to serve God even if it cost their lives.

From 1568 to1648 the French Huguenots were granted their freedom.

Pavia was the most decisive battle of the Italian Wars (1494-1529) and is considered by historians to be the first modern battle in history. The French were smashed by the Imperial army, and King Francis I was captured. This brought about the military eclipse of France and Switzerland, the century-long ascendancy of the Spanish, as well as the demise of the traditionally armed man-at-arms and the rise of hand-held firearms.

The Schmalkaldic League was a defensive league of Protestant princes in the Holy Roman Empire in the mid-sixteenth century. It received its name from the town of Schmalkalden, in Thuringia. The league was assembled by Philipp I of Hess and John Frederick, Elector of Saxony at Schmalkalden in 1531. They pledged to defend each other if their territories were attacked by Charles V, the Holy Roman Emperor. Anhalt, Bremen, Brunswick-Luneburg, Magdeburg, Mansfeld, Strassburg, and Ulm were the other original members. Constance, Reutlingen, Memmingen, Lindau, Biberach an der Rib, Isny im Allgau, and Lubeck later joined as well. The league agreed to provide 10,000 troops and 2,000 knights for their mutual protection.

In 1532 the league allied with France, and in 1538 with Denmark. The league rarely provoked Charles directly but confiscated church land, expelled bishops and Catholic princes, and helped spread Lutheranism throughout Northern Germany.

In 1544 Charles V made peace with France, with France agreeing to end their alliance with Schmalkaldic League. Charles and Pope Paul III began to gather an army in 1546, while the members of the league bickered amongst themselves, unable to unite in defense as they had originally planned. Charles defeated the league at the Battle of Muhlberg on April 24, 1547, capturing many of its leaders. However, new Protestant leagues were created, eventually leading to the Peace of Augsburg in 1555.[23]

At the end of the religious wars, religious thoughts and ideals created other Protestant denominations. Still, all the edicts and rights of existence did not allow total freedom. There had to be a government that would allow total religious expression and freedom.

It appears that there was a divine shakeup around the known world. The greater the frustration built up in people's hearts against their present government and religion, the better the New World looked in people's eyes. What a perfect time for European peoples who had many different talents and spiritual insights to converge on the land that promised freedom! This once-in-a-lifetime opportunity must be seized immediately.

THE STRUGGLES

After the thirteen colonies were formed, there ensued a great struggle for survival. Each colony belonged to a different government with different rules. Trying to establish a free society under the same bondage they came out of was distressing. They had to somehow achieve unity to pull away from what they had left: European political oppression and religious dogma.

The four major political players in the development of the New World were Britain, France, Spain, and The Netherlands. Each eventually would try to take sole possession of this new land and govern every aspect of life under one banner. As these countries struggled against each other and grew weaker as a result of the small wars, the colonies grew stronger.

The worst decision by any of the ruling factions was made by Britain in 1765. Having come into possession of all the country to the east of the Great River, King George determined to send out an army of ten thousand men to defend the colonies and have them bear a part of the expense. He attempted to collect this money by levying duties on imports and by the Stamp Tax of 1765, which taxed legal documents and printed matter. Parliament had never before taxed the American Colonies. The colonists, therefore, resisted this first attempt, raising the cry, "No taxation without representation!" They forced Parliament to repeal the Stamp Tax in 1766. However, the very next year duties were levied on paints, oils, lead, glass, and tea. Once more the colonists resisted, and, their refusal to import any goods, wares, or merchandise of English manufacture, so distressed the English that Parliament repealed every tax except that on tea. So the colonists smuggled in their tea from Holland. Deprived of the

American market, the East India Company became embarrassed and called on Parliament for aid. The company was allowed to export tea, a privilege never before granted.

Cargoes of tea were duly consigned by the East India Company to commissioners in Boston, New York, Philadelphia, and Charleston, but the people agreed not to buy any of this tea or allow it to be sold. In Boston, men disguised as Indians boarded the tea ships, overcame the guards, and destroyed the tea by throwing the boxes into the harbor. This has gone down in history as the "Boston Tea Party."[24]

As a result of this defiance, Parliament shut the port of Boston and prohibited the people of Massachusetts from functioning in local government.

BY THE

K I N G,

A

PROCLAMATION,

For Suppreſſing Rebellion and Sedition.

GEORGE *R.*

 HEREAS many of Our Subjects in divers Parts of Our Colonies and Plantations in *North America*, misled by dangerous and ill-deſigning Men, and forgetting the Allegiance which they owe to the Power that has protected and ſuſtained them, after various diſorderly Acts committed in Diſturbance of the Public Peace, to the Obſtruction of lawful Commerce, and to the Oppreſſion of Our loyal Subjects carrying on the ſame, have at length proceeded to an open and avowed Rebellion, by arraying themſelves in hoſtile Manner to withſtand the Execution of the Law, and traitorouſly preparing, ordering, and levying War againſt Us.

AND whereas there is Reaſon to apprehend that ſuch Rebellion hath been much promoted and encouraged by the traitorous Correſpondence, Counſels, and Comfort of divers wicked and deſperate Perſons within this Realm: To the End therefore, that none of Our Subjects may neglect or violate their Duty through Ignorance thereof, or through any Doubt of the Protection which the Law will afford to their Loyalty and Zeal, We have thought fit, by and with the Advice of Our Privy Council, to iſſue this Our Royal Proclamation, hereby declaring that not only all Our Officers, Civil and Military, are obliged to exert their utmoſt Endeavours

Proclamation from King George III warning the colonists that Britain has declare war against their rebellion - August 23, 1775.

Source: *William MacDonald, Documentary Source Book of American History, New York, Burt Franklin, pp. 189-190.*

The Colonists Come Together

In hopes of stamping out the rebellion among the colonists, Britain sent troops. The colonists chose George Washington to lead them in fighting against the British. Washington, a lieutenant colonel from Virginia, had great experience in battle; he was no novice at tactical fighting. In 1753 Governor Dinwiddie had sent Washington to order the French out of the Ohio Valley. In 1755 Washington advised General Edward Braddock that he could not fight wars in America like he had in France. Braddock did not listen, and the result was a massacre in which Braddock himself was killed.

The colonists were planning their move to becoming free from Britain. If America was to be independent of British rule, she needed help; but the help she needed could not come from another country only, for to ally with another country would risk losing her independence. If she wanted to be completely free, she had to trust in God's providential guidance. In hindsight, George Washington received help from God by way of a preordained victory. America had to win. As Washington reviewed his troops, he said to them, "We will win." He spoke with the same confidence as Gideon; this was Gideon's sword appearing again.[25]

As if he were being led by a force greater than the call of the colonists, Washington ingeniously led his troops to victory from 1775 to 1776. With only a comparatively few men against such a vast army of British soldiers, destiny was apparent now more than ever The British fled, and the colonies declared their independence, at this time becoming a separate state from the British government. On July 4, 1776, America officially declared her freedom from all foreign governments, but not without a great sacrifice. Many lives were lost before and after the struggles, but she held strong.

- On July 2, 1776, John Adams wrote to his wife: "The second day of July, 1776, will be the most memorable epoch in the history of America. I am apt to believe that it will be celebrated by succeeding generations as the great anniversary festival. It ought to be commemorated as the day of deliverance, by solemn acts of devotion to God Almighty. It ought to be solemnized with pomp and parade, with shows, games, sports, guns, bells, bonfires, and illuminations, from one end of this continent to the other, from this time forward forevermore."

On July 4, 1776, the Sons of Liberty celebrated their new status as American citizens by erecting a Victory or Liberty Pole.

• In a moment of urgency the Declaration of Independence was written. It began with these words: "When in the Course of human events, it becomes necessary for one people to dissolve the political bands which have connected them with another, and to assume among the Powers of the earth, the separate and equal station to which the Laws of nature and of Nature's God entitle them, a decent respect to the opinions of mankind requires that they should declare the causes which impel them to the separation.

"We hold these truths to be self-evident, that all me are created equal, that they are endowed by their Creator with certain unalienable Rights, that among these are Life, Liberty and the Pursuit of Happiness."

In nine days that saved the revolution . . . George Washington hit upon an audacious plan to turn the tide of war. On Christmas night, 1776, he led a force of 2,400 men across the ice-choked Delaware River, into the teeth of a vicious blizzard. . . . After marching all night through the storm, they attacked and defeated a garrison of 1,500 Hessian regulars at Trenton. The storm gave the American attack an element of surprise; it concealed their approach and interrupted patrols by the Hessian sentries, already exhausted from days of fending off guerilla attacks from local irregulars. A week later, having persuaded his veterans to stay past their enlistment dates through a combination of moral persuasion and a ten dollar bounty in hard coin, Washington set out to re-establish an American presence in New Jersey. Recrossing the Delaware—under conditions even worse than the first time—on January 2, 1777, Washington's men withstood a fierce counterattack by British Regulars led by General Cornwallis on the outskirts of Trenton. Seemingly trapped in their defensive position, the Americans stole away under cover of night, made a fifteen-mile march over miraculously frozen ground—the road had been knee-deep mud the day before—to Princeton. There, the exhausted troops encountered and defeated two British regiments rushing to reinforce Trenton. Victorious, Washington slipped away with his men, eventually finding winter quarters in Morristown. To the British eyes, Washington had suddenly "shown himself both a Fabius and Camillus," his march an unexpected "prodigy of generalship."[26]

On October 19, 1781, George Washington again intelligently led America to victory. At this time the British generals surrendered, and the war for sovereignty was finally over. The beginning of the American government was underway, but a tremendous amount of hard work had to be done. Many mistakes would occur; nevertheless, she was now on her own.

New Leadership

The first attempt at naming democracy was on March 1, 1781. It was called the Articles of Confederation. During two years of meetings from 1787 to 1788, a better policy was adopted; they called it the Constitution of the United State of America. It became the supreme law of the land. It was free of all past governmental laws. It established a strong and healthy national government. It would be for the people and by the people. The major concern was for the people (democracy).[27] The Constitution of the United States was like no other nation's statement of law for its government. Its primary message was to show that the God of liberty was the source of the laws by which the Constitution granted equal rights to all citizens, and made the representatives hold to the care of the people above selfish dictates, philosophies, and agendas. It granted that the people's liberty should never be in danger of being taken away.

Unlike the soaring Declaration of Independence, the Constitution of the United States promulgated neither a strict theory of governance nor a doctrine on the relationship between citizen and state, nor did it contain a ringing proclamation of national purpose. It was much simpler than that: the Constitution was a set of rules with laws to back them up. After the majestic beginning of its preamble, little poetry graced the charter; its appeal came more from ideas than from emotion. Whereas scholars may have admired the soul-stirring eloquence of Jefferson's Declaration, they treasured the rational workability of the Constitution through which men of different backgrounds but similar political principles devised the rules and built an arena of open debate over national issues. Thus the Convention not only established a government but virtually ensured that each generation would hold open debates aimed at adopting various new constitutional provisions.

In April 1789 Colonel George Washington was elected the first President of United States of America. John Adams was Vice President. Thomas Jefferson was Secretary of State. Alexander Hamilton was Secretary of the Treasury. Edmund Randolph was the Attorney General. And Henry Knox was Secretary of War. The country enjoyed economic growth. This new government led by President George Washington would allow the people to be free, free to serve God from the heart, not from edicts or an established set of religious dictates from a king. A spirit of freedom released the citizens' souls, like awakening and inhaling a breath of fresh air while listening to morning songs. This was freedom in every aspect of its definition.

After George Washington was elected the first president of the United States, he penned these words in honor of the help and provision that the God of heaven and earth had given him:

"Such being the impressions under which I have, in obedience to the public summons, repaired to the present station, it would be peculiarly improper to omit in this first official act my fervent supplications to that Almighty Being who rules over the universe, who presides in the councils of nations, and whose providential aids can supply every human defect, that His benediction may consecrate to the liberties and happiness of the people of the United States a Government instituted by themselves for these essential purposes, and may enable every instrument employed in its administration to execute with success the functions allotted to his charge. In tendering this homage to the Great Author of every public and private good, I assure myself that it expresses your sentiments not less than my own, nor those of my fellow-citizens at large less than either. No people can be bound to acknowledge and adore the Invisible Hand which conducts the affairs of men more than those of the United States. Every step by which they have advanced to the character of an independent nation seems to have been distinguished by some token of providential agency; and in the important revolution just accomplished in the system of their united government the tranquil deliberations and voluntary consent of so many distinct communities from which the event has resulted can not be compared with the means by which most governments have been established without some return of pious gratitude, along with an humble anticipation of the future blessings which the past seem to presage. These reflections, arising out of the present crisis, have forced themselves too strongly on my mind to be suppressed. You will join with me, I trust, in thinking that there are none under the influence of which the proceedings of a new and free government can more auspiciously commence."[28]

The Documents of Freedom

The new government would be led by an order ordained by a Spirit that came from above—at least that is what I believe. In 1789 in the very first Congress, James Madison submitted the Ten Amendments. They were ratified in 1791. It was called the Bill of Rights. It guaranteed Americans basic freedoms, including the rights to petition the government, to speak public opinions without fear of government reprisal, to worship freely, and to bear arms. The Tenth Amendment summed it up: "The powers not delegated to the United States by the Constitution, nor prohibited by it to the States, are reserved to the States respectively, or to the people."

Unlike the British Magna Carta, no one leader could change these laws and truths. These were laws sent from above—at least this is what I believe. The Spirit that inspired these laws gave this country an exciting impetus and made people from all walks of life part of its future success. The Founding Fathers had no idea that such a delectable meal could be so well prepared that everyone at the table could eat with joy the well-seasoned, tasty and tender law of freedom and liberty. No one could reject it, even if some in the future could not understand the "whys."

Free but not free: as America proclaimed its freedom from Britain and wrote a Declaration stating the same, not all people within its borders were free. The black Africans and the Indians were overlooked when it came to liberty and the pursuit of happiness. If all were not free then the statement, "We hold these truths . . . all men are created equal," could not be true. Therefore, in reality, it was no better than the Magna Carta. Or should we believe that the meat of the law was so inspired that those who wrote it had no idea what they were writing? If all were created equal, then the authors put blinders over their eyes in the name of free labor. But, if they truly believed that all were created equal, eventually freedom must come, because equality demanded it.

The Bill of Rights soothed the people's conscience concerning freedom under this new government, and gave hope that their civil and religious rights would not be violated. Unlike most modern countries, America's story was a story about many different people; many heads came together to share ideas, strengths, and talents. Without the input of most people in a culture, progress will stop and the culture will die. The very first colonists died and the colony with them, because they tried to enslave the only help they had. Instead of using the wisdom the Indians could provide, they destroyed their hope of survival by trying to attack and enslave them. Such was the case throughout the development of America.

With all the growing pains, the unnecessary killing of the Indians, and the bad treatment of the black Africans and their descendents, America was the fastest growing country in the world because she had brainpower built on the foundation of divine providence. Those that had wisdom took advantage of the human resources available to accomplish the jobs in a shorter and more efficient manner.

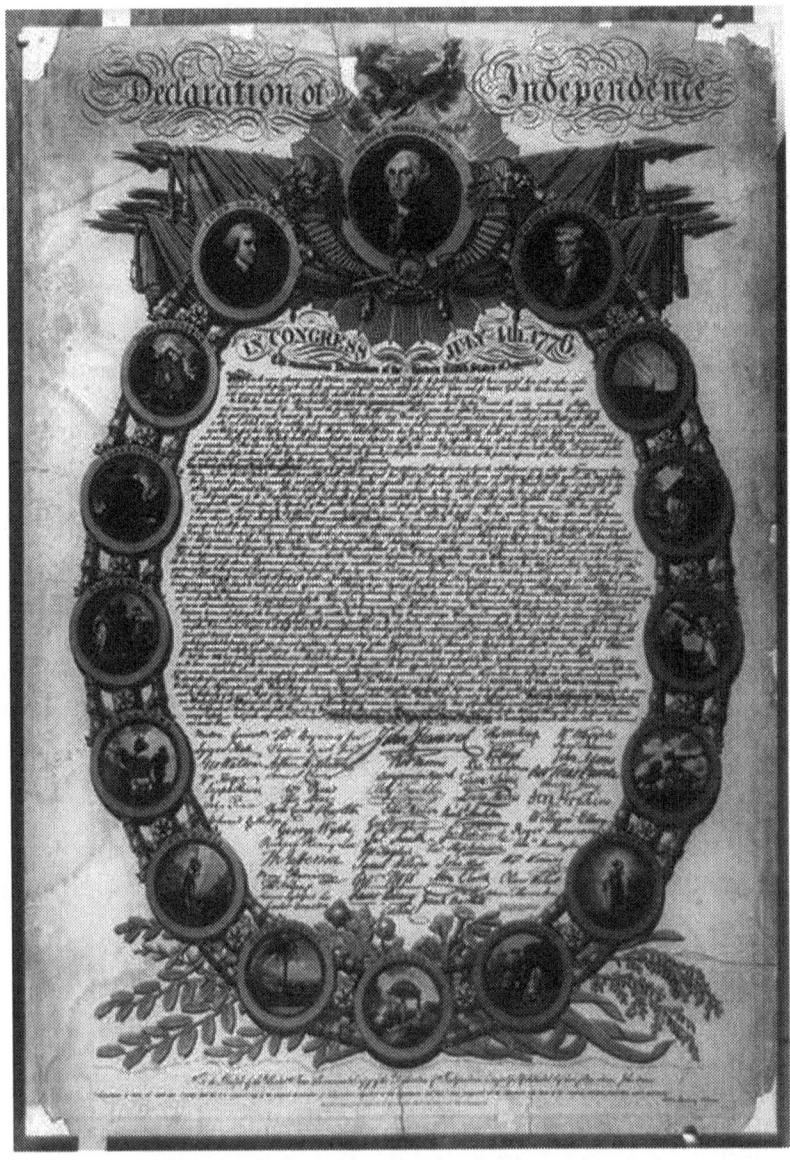

A facsimile of the Declaration of Independence, in an ornamental oval frame with medallions of seals of the thirteen original colonies, and the medallion portraits of John Hancock, George Washington, and Thomas Jefferson. Above is an eagle with shield, olive branch, and arrows, holding a streamer reading "E Pluribus Unum."[29]

THE BILL OF RIGHTS

Unalienable rights are rights people are born with, rights that cannot be taken away from them. Because of the heavy hand of the British government, the colonists did not want a strong central government; that type of government had proved to be too harsh. They wanted better treatment from their new government. As a result, a bill of rights was created:

First—granted freedom of religion, speech, press, assembly, and petition.

Second—granted the right to keep and bear arms.

Third—restricted the right of the government to locate troops in private homes.

Fourth—granted freedom from unreasonable searches and seizures.

Fifth—no person could be deprived of due process; no person could be placed in double jeopardy; no person on trial could be forced to incriminate himself.

Sixth—granted a trial by jury, the right to confront hostile witnesses, and the right to a defense lawyer in criminal cases.

Seventh—granted the right to trial by jury in civil suits of more than $20.

Eighth—prohibited excessive bail or fines and "cruel and unusual" punishment.

Ninth—made it clear that other rights, though not listed in the Constitution, would be retained by the people.

Tenth—all powers not granted to the United States or prohibited to the individual states would be kept by the states and the people.

THE ENSIGN: OUR FLAG, SYMBOL OF OUR NATION, UNITY, AND STRENGTH

As our nation was developing, wars fought on its soil in an attempt to overthrow individual states and territories. Enemies were met with the strongest of resistance called *destiny*. This country had to survive the onslaught of attack from countries that tried to proclaim part of its wealth and destiny. We fought intelligently and courageously, not knowing that the angels of God were fighting with us. Can anyone else explain why only a handful of people could keep so many enemies at bay? We lost many in our struggle but gained a nation.

After we broke away from British rule, unlike other countries, we had no banner to fight under except for spirit and heart. In 1776 a flag was created with stripes representing the thirteen original colonies and with the British emblem. It was called the Continental Colors. From 1777 to 1795 the British emblem was replaced with stars that represented each state of the thirteen colonies. As other states were added to the union, they added more stripes. Seeing that the flag would have too many stripes as other states were added, they quickly decided that the stripes would represent the thirteen original states, and stars would be added for each state that was in the union. This way each state that joined could easily be represented by another star. From 1795 to 1818, the "Star-Spangled Banner" was born.

Continental Colors-1776

"The Star Spangled Banner"
By Francis Scott Key

Oh, say can you see by the dawn's early light
What so proudly we hailed at the twilight's last gleaming?
Whose broad stripes and bright stars through the perilous fight,
O'er the ramparts we watched were so gallantly streaming?
And the rockets' red glare, the bombs bursting in air,
Gave proof through the night that our flag was still there.
Oh say, does that Star-Spangled Banner yet wave
O'er the land of the free and the home of the brave?

On the shore, dimly seen through the mists of the deep,
Where the foe's haughty host in dread silence reposes,
What is that which the breeze, o'er the towering steep,
As it fitfully blows, half conceals, half discloses?
Now it catches the gleam of the morning's first beam,
In full glory reflected now shines in the stream:
'Tis the Star-Spangled Banner! Oh long may it wave
O'er the land of the free and the home of the brave!

And where is that band who so vauntingly swore
That the havoc of war and the battle's confusion,
A home and a country should leave us no more?
Their blood has washed out their foul footsteps' pollution.
No refuge could save the hireling and slave
From the terror of flight, or the gloom of the grave:
And the Star-Spangled banner in triumph doth wave
O'er the land of the free and the home of the brave!

Oh! thus be it ever, when freemen shall stand
Between their loved home and the war's desolation!
Blest with vict'ry and peace, may the heav'n rescued land
Praise the Pow'r that hath made and preserved us a nation.
Then conquer we must, when our cause it is just,
And this be our motto: "In God is our trust."
And the Star-Spangled Banner in triumph shall wave
O'er the land of the free and the home of the brave!

CHAPTER 7
FLAG PATTERN ACCEPTED

As a young girl in Philadelphia, Elizabeth Griscom showed considerable aptitude for fine needlework. She married John Ross in 1773, worked with him in his upholsterer's shop, and carried on the business after he was killed in 1776 while serving in the military.

According to her grandson, William Canby, in a paper presented in 1870, George Washington, Robert Morris, and George Ross visited Betsy Ross in June 1776 and asked her to design an ensign. (George Ross was her late husband's uncle.) The legend is that they asked her to make a flag for the new nation that would declare its independence the following month. Incorporating her suggestions, Washington redrew a rough sketch and presented it to her. Betsy Ross then fashioned the flag in her back parlor.[30] On June 14, 1777, the Continental Congress adopted the Stars and Stripes as the national flag of the United States.[31]

Because the history books are closed, we will reverently accept this story as true and declare that Betsy Ross gave us our flag that we presently call "Old Glory."

After the Declaration of Independence was signed, almost a year passed before Congress adopted a new flag. But variations in the flag persisted, and changes continued during much of the nineteenth century. The Flag Act of 1818 fixed the number of horizontal stripes at thirteen and gave the president the authority to determine the star arrangement. The United States Army did not carry the now-familiar stars and stripes into battle until the Mexican War in 1846.

Finally in 1912, an executive order defined the design of the flag, including the star arrangement. Later, when Alaska and Hawaii entered the Union, stars representing those states were added to the flag, adopting the traditional horizontal arrangement.

American involvement in the Spanish-American War, World War I, and World War II stimulated patriotic sentiments and interest in the flag. In 1942 Congress established rules and customs concerning the flag and the Pledge of Allegiance.

The years since World War II have seen the refinement of various laws and regulations concerning the flag. Today it has become an accepted part of the decoration of most public buildings and a symbol regarded as appropriate for almost any setting where citizens assemble.

Betsey [sic] Ross sewing the flag.[32]

The Betsy Ross Design

The present flag of the United State of America

"She Cries Aloud—Freedom!"
By Jocelyn Stewart

Silhouetting against Heaven's scenes
From sunrise to sunset
The title deed of Freedom waves
As a reminder
Lest we forget
The expense of our Liberty
Old Glory embodies a country's quest
From thirteen British colonies
To a World leader
It is the symbol of our nation's Unity
Its genesis
Is directly relative to the nation's journey
Crimson symbolic for Hardness and Valor
The alternating white stripes
Purity and Innocence
Betsy Ross skillfully tailored
Fifty stars staggering on a field of blue
For Vigilance, Perseverance, and Justice
Inanimate
Yet it voices
A profound philosophy
Represents the eternal principles of Justice and Harmony
It is an appeal to a true God
And proclaims the fearless Courage
Of soldiers then and now
Dedicated to the preservation of Liberty
Both personal and religious
The American Flag extends an invitation to a destiny
Secured by self sacrifice and devotion
Patriotism is more than pertinent
It exceeds ceremonial reverence
And recitations of the Pledge of Allegiance

We are cognizant of its indubitable intent
Thus with hands over indebted hearts
We swear our piety
To Liberty, Justice, Unity
As the Flag of the United States stands guard

Why do we need a flag? We need a flag to show other nations that we are unified and strong. The stars and the stripes represent where we came from, where we are now, and where we are going. Fifty states are led by one president, whose executive powers are checked and balanced by both the judicial and legislative branches of the United States government. When a leader or a delegate of this country goes into a foreign country, he or she goes under the authority of the stars and stripes. When we are in a military conflict, we take with us the stars and stripes. The only flag in the world that every other country can unmistakably identify is the stars and stripes of the United States of America. Our flag is not known because of its colors; the colors are known because of the Christ-like spirit to give to others even while we are bombing their country in retaliation for crimes committed against us. Be proud of your country. This is a good country. We are blessed by God.

FLAG FOLDING CEREMONY

The flag-folding ceremony described by the Uniformed Services is a dramatic and uplifting way to honor the flag on special days, such as Memorial Day or Veterans Day, and is sometimes used at retirement ceremonies. Here is a typical sequence of the ceremony.

The flag-folding ceremony represents the religious principles on which our country was originally founded. The portion of the flag-denoting honor is the canton of blue containing the stars representing the states under which our veterans served in uniform. The canton field of blue dresses from left to right and is inverted when draped as a pall on a casket of a veteran who has served our country in uniform.

In the Armed Forces of the United States, at the ceremony of retreat the flag is lowered, folded in a triangular fold, and kept under watch throughout the night as a tribute to our nation's honored dead. The next morning it is brought out and, at the ceremony of reveille, run aloft as a symbol of our belief in the resurrection of the body.

1. The first fold of our flag symbolizes life.

2. The second fold symbolizes our belief in eternal life.

3. The third fold honors and remembers the veteran departing our ranks who gave a portion of his or her life for the defense of our country to attain peace throughout the world.

4. The fourth fold represents our weaker nature, for as American citizens trusting in God, it is to Him we turn in times of peace as well as in times of war for His divine guidance.

5. The fifth fold is a tribute to our country, for in the words of Stephen Decatur, "Our country, in dealing with other countries, may she always be right; but it is still our country, right or wrong."

6. The sixth fold is for where our hearts lie. With our heart we pledge allegiance to the flag of the United States of America and to the republic for which it stands, one nation, under God, indivisible, with liberty and justice for all.

7. The seventh fold is a tribute to our Armed Forces, for they protect our country and our flag against all her enemies, whether they be found within or without the boundaries of our republic.

8. The eighth fold is a tribute to the mother who entered into the valley of the shadow of death that we might see the light of day, and to honor her for whom the flag flies on Mother's Day.

9. The ninth fold is a tribute to womanhood; for it has been through her faith, love, loyalty, and devotion that the characters of the men and women who have made this country great have been molded.

10. The tenth fold is a tribute to father, for he, too, has given his sons and daughters for the defense of our country.

11. The eleventh fold, in the eyes of a Hebrew citizen, represents the lower portion of the seal of King David and King Solomon and glorifies, in their eyes, the God of Abraham, Isaac, and Jacob.

12. The twelfth fold, in the eyes of a Christian citizen, represents an emblem of eternity and glorifies, in their eyes, God the Father, the Son, and Holy Ghost.

When the flag is completely folded, the stars are uppermost, reminding us of our national motto, "In God We Trust." After it is completely folded and tucked in, the flag takes on the appearance of a cocked hat, ever reminding us of the soldiers who served under General George Washington and the sailors and marines who served under Captain John Paul Jones who were followed by their comrades and shipmates in the Armed Forces of the United States, preserving for us the rights, privileges, and freedoms we enjoy today.[33]

SALUTE OUR GREATNESS

To *salute* means "to give a sign of respect, courtesy, or goodwill to; to express commendation of; to show honor to one's country or a person in command, such as a military officer." In 1977 I enlisted in the United States Navy. I learned to salute all officers. I learned to salute the flag whenever it was being hoisted. While the ceremonies were enacted, I stood there with my arm raised, my elbow bent so that my right forearm pointed my hand to the right tip of my Navy hat. I was honoring, respecting, and showing loyalty to the country I had sworn to protect from enemies, foreign and domestic.

It is a shame for me to see Americans dishonor the flag while it is being hoisted during different ceremonies or activities in which we are engaged. When I hear the words, "All rise for the National Anthem," I am displeased and disappointed when I turn around and see children sitting with their hands folded as if to say, "I defy this country." Then I see adults who keep their hats on, with a defiant look in their countenance toward the greatness of our country. In 1996 the National Basketball Association (NBA) suspended one of its players for not standing while the National Anthem was being played. The player had converted to Islam and felt that to stand in honor of this country because of its previous treatment of the African slaves was disrespectful to his new religion. He also stated he could not honor America because he believed this to be a country of repression. He thought he had a right to protest, but others also had a right to protest against his actions. The rule of the NBA is that all players must stand during the playing of the National Anthem; this is in the contract between the NBA players and the association.

The National Anthem honors the flag that honors the country. It was very offensive for an American to disrespect his own country in front of the whole nation. That little sit-down cost him more than he possibly could have imagined. Regardless of our past history, Americans come together when we are mocked. To disrespect our flag is to attack each and every citizen that stands behind the banner that represents who we are as a nation.

People who remain seated during a public ceremony while the National Anthem is being played or sung and the Pledge of Allegiance is being recited are stating by their actions that they disrespect this country. There is no other way to construe it. It only takes a small amount of effort to stand, remove your cap, and place your hand over your heart to honor the country that is giving you the privilege to participate in the event of the moment.

WHY DO THEY HATE US—
INTERNAL AND EXTERNAL

In existence from 1776 to 2007, as young as this country is we are the most advanced. This is seen in our buildings, our houses, our stores, our technology, our livelihood, our manufacturing (domestic or abroad), our love for the Lord Jesus Christ, our acceptance of others' lifestyles, our freedom of speech, the beauty of our land, our generosity, our willingness to sacrifice the lives of military personnel so others may be free, our boldness to declare our strength, our love for Israel, and most of all the Preamble in the Declaration of Independence. We have the resources to do what other people and countries can only dream of. Because of us other countries exist and prosper; whenever disaster strikes, we give our helping hands. Most of the time, we are the only hands. Because of and in spite of these and other blessings, we are often hated.

It should be a crime to burn the flag that represents your nation. Your nation represents you, your family, your culture, your beliefs, and your values. We may not agree with every decision that is made by our federal, state, and local governments, but we have a duty to respect their laws. In this country we have the right to voice our disagreement through different media, but we do not have the right to commit a crime against any to show our disagreement. How many of you would set fire to your home, your cars, or destroy any of your personal property? When I see Americans burn their own country's flag, I see confused people who are controlled by evil and self-destructive forces. A person who burns the flag is saying to the government, "I can't burn down the whole country, my family, or way of life, so I'm burning the flag." But by burning the flag, you are symbolically destroying your freedoms while at the same time we are trying to liberate certain countries to give them a life of freedom. When these same countries burn our flag, they are burning the very hands that are liberating them. Yet if we do not help them, they will blame us for that. It seems to be a no-win situation.

Each citizen should understand one important thing about the flag of their country: it represents their citizenship. Because we are citizens of America, the flag is ours. It is not just a government's flag; it is the citizens' flag. It flies over our schools, churches, municipals buildings, our sports facilities, and our government buildings. It is posted and painted on our cars, buses, trains, and planes. It was taken to the moon and Mars.

When other counties are in distress and need help, how many flags from different countries are present? Not too many. Even if some others are present, you will consistently see the Stars and Stripes. Just imagine if the Stars and Stripes were not at most disasters in the world: many people that are saved alive would not have gotten that second chance at life. The countries themselves would be in ruin. America, with all of its many help organizations, has supported countries struck by disaster with food, water, clothing, food, medicine, money, and even blood. Our programs to feed the hungry are the largest in the world. We transcend the word *help* when others in this world are in need. Our flag symbolizes help and care.

CHAPTER 8
PLEDGE OF ALLEGIANCE

For Americans and citizens of all countries, pledging allegiance is something we must all do in order to secure and ensure the common welfare of the people and protect the land in which we live from foreign and domestic enemies. Every statement of commitment has a philosophy that is accepted by the population at large, but which a small portion of the population wants to change. The latter is the enemy. All things except the laws of God are subject to change, but the people of a democratic government whose law is shaped by God's moral law must be careful not to make changes concerning the moral things that hold a democratic society together. Democracy is for the people and by the people. History has proven time and again that manmade laws are opinions that can be changed by the next person who assumes the office. There are no absolutes when it comes to man's laws; therefore, to constantly change laws in order to find that one law everyone agrees with is death to a nation. The moral laws of God are absolute, and they bring security. The government that has these laws will have a peaceful society. Conversely, if the people opt for man's law they will be subject to man's philosophy, which is like the seas driven by angry winds. When human philosophy replaces divine moral laws, all under its jurisdiction become unstable. The script that we use for pledging allegiance has a body, soul, and spirit of dedication that is governed by God's principles.

The original Pledge of Allegiance—"I pledge allegiance to my flag and the Republic for which it stands, one nation, indivisible, with liberty and justice for all,"—was written in September of 1892, by Francis Bellamy for *The Youth's Companion* magazine in Boston. The phrase was printed on leaflets and sent to schools throughout the United States.

The first organized use of the Pledge of Allegiance came on October 12, 1892, when approximately 12 million American school children recited it to commemorate the four- hundred-year anniversary of Columbus's voyage. In 1923 the first National Flag Conference in Washington, D.C., voted to change the words *my flag* to "the flag of the United States of America." Congress officially recognized the Pledge of Allegiance in 1942, but in 1943 the Supreme Court ruled that public school students could not be forced to recite it.

The words "under God" were added in 1954 by then President Eisenhower, who stated at the time, "In this way we are reaffirming the transcendence of religious faith in America's heritage and future; in this way we shall constantly strengthen those spiritual weapons which forever will be our country's most powerful resource in peace and war."

I pledge allegiance to the Flag, of the United States of America and to the Republic for which it stands, One Nation under God Indivisible, with Liberty and Justice for All.

The Pledge of Allegiance has gone through many positive changes to help strengthen the American people's faith in this country; however, many people do not support this ideal. They do not understand the connection between the call of this great nation and the faith of the people in it. If it were their choice, they would remove all references of God from our vocabulary. They are ignorant of the fact that they are a minority in this regard. Most Americans believe in God. We brought the worship of our

God with us from Israel into the New World. We shared our God with the native Indians that we discovered here and with the African slaves that were brought here. We openly glorified God when we declared independence from Great Britain. We used the wisdom of God to establish our laws and national policies. We commemorated God on our currency, both coin and paper. We have made God chief judge, and His commandments preside over every one of our courtrooms. Why would we now want to remove God from the expressions of our heritage and culture? If a country as great and pleasant as America would be conquered by another, and its citizens taken away into a foreign land, the citizens would say like the psalmist in the Bible, "If I forget you, O Jerusalem, let my right hand forget its skill" (Psalm 137:5)

Many people like Dr. John W. Baer, Charles Johnson of Utah, Michael Newdow, and others do not understand the connection between the call of this country's government into existence, the words that make up the Preamble, and the words that make up the Pledge of Allegiance. These men call themselves atheists and would like all references of God removed from any articles in America that bear His name. These men know that most Americans believe in God, but it is their intention to divide us so they can create a morality war. They want to destroy the fabric of truth that holds us together. It is not coincidental how the meaning and purpose of the U. S. Constitution is consistent with all the patriotic symbols that we as a nation hold dear to us. The term *God* is found in everything we do. The natives that were here from the beginning acknowledged God. God was mentioned when Columbus was commissioned to sail the Atlantic looking for India. God was mentioned when this land was colonized by the British government. Finally, God was mentioned when we declared independence by defeating the British government. Why then would all these so-called legislative officers want to pass laws that would remove the word *God* from our vocabulary? It is very simple: they are ignoring our history.

These men and women that seek to remove the godly principles from our foundation should never be granted the right to remove something so true and invigorating from this country. The legislators that vote to pass laws in favor of Mr. Newdow and other God haters feel they are instituting a philosophy of "political correctness." They don't realize that they are bringing destruction to their own homes. They call it *patriotism*. This deduction, they think, will help everyone, thereby making them patriotic. How will they explain to their own sons and daughters what it means to be patriotic when a rebel solicits them to rebel against their own country? If there is no consciousness of godliness, then there is no reason not to rebel.

Do these people, who have not given a particle of hope for positive change in this great country, feel they can—overnight, or in any span of time—change the fiber of what we believe? They want to change our country in the name of "no more religion—leave me alone so I may practice lawlessness and immorality without having God goading my conscience, making me feel guilty." As long as there are churches in this country, the legislators will not be able to remove the only name (Jesus) that helps keep us morally straight. There is no other name given to us that is able to bring peace.

One of O. J. Simpson's famed lawyers, Alan Dershowitz, a graduate of Yale Law School, wrote a book to inform people that they do not need God or religion to be good or to act right. I agree with him on this one point: people do not need religion; however, they *do* need the Lord Jesus Christ (God). Hey Allen, try telling your theory to Ted Bundy, O. J. Simpson, Michael Ross, the Son of Sam (David Berkowitz), and all the human beings who have been convicted of committing a heinous crime. Try convincing the many women who were raped by family men. Try selling this line to children who were molested by family members that were highly esteemed by the community. Try telling this to the many grieving families of the victims of these crimes.

Before Ted Bundy was executed on January 24, 1989, he requested an interview with Dr. James Dobson. In that interview he explained how he left his Christian upbringing in favor of his own way of living. This rejection of God-consciousness led to the deaths of many innocent women, and his last victim was a twelve-year-old girl.

After Michael Ross was convicted and sentenced to die, he wrote journals, which can be located on the Web under "Michael Ross." Michael stated that he wished he could do it over again by following God instead of rejecting Him.

David Berkowitz killed many women in New York. After his arrest, he calmly described each murder to Sergeant Joseph Coffey. He also confessed to being a Satanist, one who has no God-consciousness. After many years in prison, David confessed to receiving the Lord Jesus Christ in his life. Only after his conversion did he regret that he had not had God in his conscience.[34] These men testified that if they had a God consciousness living in them, they would not have committed these crimes.

The sad thing about people like Alan Dershowitz is that they promote a conscience of human guidance, which has already proven to be deadly from all angles of life. Human guidance failed Marilyn Monroe. It failed Hitler. It failed Michael Ross. It failed Jesse Jackson, Bill Clinton, and it failed me. Since Alan Dershowitz has decided to put down God-consciousness, he must understand that his philosophy of humanism is what causes lawyers to lie when they know the truth. I am not talking about lawyer-client privileges. I am addressing outright lying. Maybe this is why some groups want to remove the wording "under God" from the Pledge of Allegiance. By removing this godly phrase, they feel they can do wrong and not feel guilty about it, or do that which is considered right and get accolades for it. Either way, they feel they are not held responsible for their actions.

This is not Caesar's government where there is no truth and each person lives by the law of his own conscience. The religious practices of Rome were based on pluralistic beliefs. All of their ideological gods controlled their daily activities. Caesar himself was considered a god, but he worshiped gods made by the hand of men. He implemented his own laws while yet unsure of what his own soul was following. There was no justice for all; justice was determined by the emotion of Caesar. There was no true love because every man had his own belief about love.

The god of fertility ruled the sexual expressions of Caesar's government. Brothers married sisters, and a brother would take his own brother's wife. A man could kill his own mother. There was no family loyalty. Caesar's government had plenty of gods, but not the true God to guide their behavior and call them into question regarding their action. Immorality was paramount, and lust and greed drove them to spiritual and economical destruction. They cheated their bodies, their homes, their families, their friends, and their government. A society in which there is no God-consciousness is in the whirlwind of destruction. They will fall hard and break into too many pieces like Humpty Dumpty, and no one will be able to put them back together again. America does not need this.

If people live their life believing only what they think, they are foolish and will fall like Humpty Dumpty. Their fall will be great, and they will never find truth. It is evident that no man possesses truth. Truth can only be found in Christ because Christ is the truth. Let us learn from Caesar's government that God-conscious people, even though not perfect, are moral people who care for the welfare of other people. Alan Dershowitz and others like him have no rehabilitating laws that will change the sinful nature of men to make them better citizens. How then can they say that no one needs God? Hypotheses like Dershowitz's prove only one thing: a person can spend thousands of dollars to be educated in a great learning institution but never come to the knowledge of the truth.

We need God, and we will continue to acknowledge Him at all times. What we do not need is a book written by a self-serving humanistic educator that tries to persuade Americans not to trust in the God of Creation. Humanity has served God from the beginning of time. Does Dershowitz really think that within the short period of his life he is going to convince the entire population to turn from God? *I don't think so.* He may be able to brainwash some of these humanist radio talk show hosts and some self-proclaimed atheists who do not have a clue about life in the first place. However, we, the majority, will and must continue to acknowledge God.

Our pledge to the flag goes deeper than putting the hand over the heart or taking the hat off the head or raising the arm to put the fingertip to the hat. It is a way of life. Because of this pledge, many men and women have given their lives to protect this country and secure the freedom of other counties. If we look into the spirit of the Pledge of Allegiance, we will find extremely valuable antidotes that can be used as both political and civil medicine. Once they are used, they can heal and help us respect most of our differences. My personal interpretation of the Pledge of Allegiance evokes a picture of a clear and present safety pavilion. I can only hope that this is a revelation for me and all who will accept this elementary interpretation.

I

I—a personal pronoun that speaks of self; one's character, volition, ambition, and purpose. It represents one person alone. The reason the Pledge of Allegiance starts with *I* is to show individual responsibility.

No other individual besides me is responsible for my actions and character. What I do reflects solely on me, but it may be a praise or a dishonor that reflects on those who are close to me. As an adult, my every action should be motivated by my own volition. I should not blame mother, father, sister, brother, relative, other ethnic groups, wind, or rain for my actions. However, many times adults, because of the abuse and ill teaching they received as children, have severe scars that cause us to empathize with their erroneous behavior.

When a child exhibits good behavior, it could be contributive to wholesome up-bringing. This quality of behavior should always be praised. There are times when a child is reared the proper way but fails to hold to that teaching. This contrary lifestyle should never be blamed on wholesome up-bringing. We should praise others for helping us get through our difficult adolescent years. As an adult I should have full control over my emotions so that I may live peaceably with all men. I must act virtuously. I must not destroy the fiber of my family, country, or friends. *I*, not someone else, am the key to success in a true, free, democratic society. It is wrong to take away the liberty of others and to withhold from them the rights afforded by God. Any person in the past or the present that does such a thing is evil. We have a mandate to do the godly thing, and the responsibility rests with *me*. If *I* do not do it, then only I am to blame. If people join evil groups that are out to destroy this country, then once those groups are punished the individuals in those groups have no one to blame but themselves.

Twin, triplet, and quadruplet babies may be born during a span of minutes or hours from the same womb, but as they grow into the stage of accountability, each one must give an account as an individual.

Government members belong to a particular political party. They must look at themselves to see if they are promoting and doing what is right. They must say to themselves, am I doing the right thing, or am I following my party's opinions? If the party's opinions are wrong and they go along with it, they must take responsibility for their own actions. No one should say, "I did it because everybody else did it." Mindless conformity does not excuse the action. However, there are times when threats to their lives may cause them to follow the crowd. It does not happen often, but we have to be fair and mention the exceptions; this exception is only for adults. Children, however, sometimes will follow the crowd. Let us hope the crowd gives sound, moral advice.

We live in an age in which guilty criminals are justified in their criminal activities; for example, they may be represented by a defense attorney that presents a strong, convincing argument to show that they were injected with the disease of child abuse, which caused them to act out their aggression on the hapless victim. While it is true and clear that habits forced on children do create abnormal characteristics in adults, it does not take away from the "I" theory. An adult individual must be held responsible for his or her own actions.

Pledge Allegiance

Pledge means "a promise or agreement to do or forbear." The key word is *promise*.

Allegiance means "devotion or loyalty to a person, group, or cause." The synonym is *fidelity*. The key word is *devotion*.

Devotion means "ardent love or affection." The promise to devote oneself is a very powerful characteristic to have when one has a good reason for that devotion.

Expect means "to consider probable or certain." We are expected to act with devotion to that which is truly right and good. The expectation we have of others should not be greater or less than what we require of ourselves.

Pledge allegiance means "a promise to give oneself with a sure affection of trust and loyalty, declaring to others that with fidelity one will perform one's obligations." The military under the command of the Commander in Chief has the responsibility of protecting this country from foreign and domestic enemies. When men and women join this elite group of dedicated Americans, they do it on a volunteer basis with the understanding that they may have to sacrifice their lives. The enemies of this country hate this type of allegiance.

Even though the 1954 law stated that children should not be forced to recite the Pledge of Allegiance, that law defeated the purpose of maintaining devoted youths who would comprise a military that enemies fear. Children should learn the Pledge of Allegiance, whether the process is called "force" or "by rote." They should practice it until it is branded on their hearts and brains. Some governments teach their children to hate other people because they are "infidels" and must be killed. They teach them that they must kill the enemy even if they have to blow themselves up to do it. They call it the "greater good." I fail to see what is so good about ending your own life when the purpose is futile. If evil governments are willing to indoctrinate children to do evil, then we should be willing to instill in our children a pledge that seeks the good of the world.

Why do our country's enemies wish to practice "pledging allegiance removal" on children before they reach adulthood? The answer is simply stated in the definition. Our enemies understand the power of meanings. Therefore, they cunningly try to remove the Pledge of Allegiance from the primary grades. Removing devotion from children's development could cause them as adults to bomb our federal buildings and kill innocent children, then call it collateral damages. Just imagine what this country will be like in the next few years once the effects of devotion and dedication are removed from our children's hearts and thinking. Take a look at the conditions of our schools. Police have to body search students to prevent them from bringing knives and guns into the schools. This is not a small-scale occurrence; this is on a larger scale. If we can put the attitude of pledging allegiance to do good to all men in the hearts of our children and youths, it will stop many of the unnecessary intentional murders that occur year after year. As long as there is the conscious pledging of allegiance to good and for goodness' sake, there will be loyalty to that which the pledge is directed.

To the Flag of the United States of America
To the Republic for Which It Stands

A flag is an emblem that represents a country, state, city, or province. Whether a country is strong or weak, the flag represents its character. The United States flag is a beautiful attraction and is a statement of our freedom and strength for all to see. Saluting this flag is a noble and patriotic obligation. "This land is my land," so the song goes. Therefore, the obligation we have is to protect what we own. By saluting the flag, we are claiming ownership.

Love for country is a godly character trait. Heaven belongs to God; therefore, He takes care of it. God made this earth for us and said it was good. He told us to have dominion over it. We do not worship this country, but we should love it, and it is our responsibility to care for it. By honoring the flag, we show honor to the country. As citizens of the United States of America, our primary obligation is to this country.

"A republic is a commonwealth; a state in which the supreme power is vested in elected representatives."[35] Every state, county, city, and territory owned by this republic is embodied in the flag. By pledging allegiance to the flag, we pledge allegiance to each citizen, regardless of the geographical location in which they may live.

Our republic is a land of freedom, strength, and wealth. Our republic is a land where religious expression is accepted. It protects people of different sexual preferences. Our republic provides for the elderly (within means). The flag stands for what our republic stands for. It stands for our style of government. It stands for redress. It stands for our "checks and balances" system, which holds our powers together as one nation.

Every nation has internal problems, even a theocratic one. America has its share of problems as well. Despite the imperfections of the political and religious leaderships, this country is still the greatest country in the world. We must pledge our allegiance if we want to see morality permeate our system. When we salute the flag, we are saluting the republic that the flag represents.

One Nation under God

From the decree to set sail to India to the Pilgrims landing in Massachusetts, the establishment of this country's government is believed to have been ordained by God. A nation was formed as a result of written laws being established by a group of people that appointed one executive leader. Supporting subordinates surrounded that leader. That nation had cities, territories, principalities, and states under its rule, but it was still one nation. Regardless of the names of the individual states, they are all under God. Without argument, God does exist. He is real. Whether a person is willing to acknowledge Him or not, He is real. From the creation of the world, He is supreme and He is sovereign. In the matter of geography, heaven is where He resides.

The heavens are located above the earth. Anyone with intelligence will have no problem with this truth. A blind person would be able to tell anyone that the heavens are above the earth. One does not need religion to acknowledge the fact that the heavens are above the earth. Then why is it that some people fight the statement, "One nation under God"?

Astronomers study the heavens. They study the stars, the moons, and the sun. They study constellations and galaxies. Mythology, as fallible as it is, is a schoolmaster to teach us about the heavens. The belief system of mythology taught us that the gods resided in a place called heaven, which was above the earth. Poets and classical writers often refer to the stars in the heavens. When Columbus came to the New World, he found the natives worshiping the supreme gods from the heavens.

Religion is man's way of trying to find God. It includes all type of rituals and practices; some are good and some are not so good. Some are bad, and some are very bad. Religion is the opiate of the soul. It is intangible because it deals primarily with the mind and the soul. These last two are real, however intangible. Despite your dedication and commitment to your religious faith, you were not born with a religion; you were born male or female.

Once you die and your body is decomposed, anthropologists can only identify you as male or female by your skeletal remains. But a religious title is something someone adopts for you, or that you adopt for yourself. If you are called by a certain religion, you attach that title to yourself. The religion I acknowledge is Pentecostal Apostolic. I was not born under this title; I adopted it in 1977 after being saved and water baptized in the name of Jesus Christ and Spirit baptized with the Holy Spirit. Religion is good if it supports freedom for all human beings. It must tolerate the animal kingdom as well. However, God is not a religion; He is not Baptist, Pentecostal, Apostolic, Catholic, Methodist, Lutheran, Jew, Moslem, Hindus, Buddhist, Zionist or any other religion. God is a Spirit; He is real, and He is in the heavens above the earth. From the beginning of civilization to the present and in every existing country there is an absolute belief that the gods dwell in heaven. Even though people worship many false gods, there is no controversy about where the nation is positioned in relation to where the gods dwell. If nonexistent gods are considered to have their home in the heavens, how much more does the true God have His home in the heavens?

All of our Founding Fathers believed in the God of heaven. Regardless of their relationship with Him, they all knew where the Most High dwelled; He was in heaven, and they were on earth. Therefore, they were one nation under God. Our pledge to our nation acknowledges that our nation is under God because God is in heaven. Our government should not remove a principle and a truth from the Pledge of Allegiance to satisfy a small number of people who get offended by the word *God*. Maybe they would prefer these phrases: "One nation under Hitler. One nation under Stalin. One nation under David Dukes. One nation under Lewis Farrakhan. One nation under Edi Amin." Or maybe a more patriotic category of persons would suit: "One nation under Abraham Lincoln, or John F. Kennedy, or Martin Luther King Jr." Unfortunately, they cannot have one nation under any of these men because they were on the earth and earthly. Though powerful, they could not direct the course of the world. Only God has the power to be on the earth and over it at the same time. Only He can direct the course this world, our nation, and our lives.

Maybe the gainsayers would like the phrase, "One nation over the devil," or, "One nation under the devil." The devil is below the earth. Even Hollywood knows where the devil resides. In all of their films and books, they depict the devil as being under the earth. But they always depict God and His angels as being over the earth.

The word *over* in this context also acknowledges the divine guidance of God for this country. His supreme power and protection show that He is over us to cover us. This is why we sing "God Bless America." To be *over* is always to have subjects looking up as a sign of submission. God is over us like a boss to whom we have to answer. He has the final say. The majority of the people in this country believe in God regardless of their religious affiliation. Therefore, it is not an immoral or uncivil thing to recite, "One nation under God."

God is *over* us; therefore, He sets laws, rules, and commandments. He has more than just Ten Commandments; the other commandments derive from the original ten. There is security in following the moral laws of God. If we are moral creatures as we say we are, then following the guidelines of God's moral commandments should not be a problem. Very few humans like to be labeled as "immoral." To illustrate my point, our human bodies contain 75 percent water, so it should not be a problem to be called water-drinking creatures. We need water to survive. For those of us who do not obey the "law" of putting water in and on our bodies, the violations have consequences. The consequence for not putting water in and on our bodies is that we will smell bad or die. If violating the commandment of using water has bad consequences, then I must submit to you that all are bad. In like manner, if we do not obey the moral laws of God, the laws themselves will punish us. If one of the Ten Commandments is wrong for us to follow, then I must summit to you that all are bad. However, the laws are not bad; they are good for us. To acknowledge that God is over us is to enjoy the blessings of good moral behavior.

In the same regard, *under* means "servitude, trampling underfoot, belittlement, and subordination." The devil, because of his lack of values and morals, is seen as beneath us. It is a fact that the majority of people do not see themselves as being in bondage to or under the control of such an attitude and character. So it is not fitting to have a man or the devil as a symbol of authority over us. All nations are under God, and we are just one of those nations under Him. So it is appropriate for us to say, "One nation under God."

After Hurricane Katrina and her sister Rita twisted and twirled their way through Louisiana, Alabama, and Texas, causing many deaths and billons of dollars in damages, Jay Leno asked on his nightly television show, "Are we sure this is a good time to take God out of the Pledge of Allegiance?" After so much proof that God is real, after so much evidence that God pieced together this country, it would not be a good thing to remove His name from His own work. Neither would it be appropriate if we removed the Founding Fathers' signatures from the Declaration of Independence.

Indivisible

Indivisible means "undivided, indispensable, essential, and complete." The motto that is used for our flag tells other nations and ourselves that we will not be divided when trouble comes. We will stand together as one unit. After our country was attacked on September 11, 2001, we came together as one. The Democrats, Republicans, Independents, Whites, Blacks, Indians, rich, poor, good, bad, educated, uneducated, weak, strong, children, adults, sports stars, police, firefighters, and religious institutions all stood hand in hand, regardless of their differences, stating they were completely united in purpose to defend this country. Our first thought was to raise the flag above whatever we had going on in our lives to protect what was most important at that time: human life.

It occurred to Osama bin Laden and others that they could drive a wedge between the different factions of our nation. How wrong they were! That violent act, like the one perpetrated on Pearl Harbor in 1941, only strengthened us and created a resolve that caused young men and women to enlist in the military from all walks of American life. These enlistees' essential purposes were to hunt down the enemy terrorists and to keep this country and our way of life safe. These acts showed that we were not divided as the enemy thought we were. Our colors are red, white and blue, and these colors "don't run." We are indivisible.

With Liberty and Justice for All

Liberty—with fragrance sweeter than roses and luster brighter than gold—is the quintessential lifestyle in the U. S. A. We love the fact that we have the right to take a walk in the cool of the night. We love the fact that we can continue our education and choose a career based on our individual aspiration and inspiration. We love the fact that our women and children are considered human beings and not property. They are human beings created equally with a soul. Each one of us, if financially capable and if the seller and the realtor are not prejudiced, can buy land and other properties. Our flag represents the great opportunities for everyone in this country.

The pledge includes justice for all. Our history does not show fidelity in this respect; however, the spirit to fight for the rights given to those that were oppressed was written in black and white. The flag represents the clear judicial processes in our courts of justice. If accused of a crime, people are innocent until proven guilty, and the outcome is determined in court by a jury of peers. We do not have a Ku Klux Klan vigilante system; we have a jurisprudence system based on fair principles. Our law enforcers do not have the right to execute judgment; therefore, both the criminal and the innocent should feel safe while in their custody. (At least this is the way it *should* be.)

The justice decree of the pledge extends into our corporate and our athletic systems. The United States is like no other country in the world that extends justice to all of it citizens. We extend our justice to citizens that were born in others countries by allowing them to request a change to the Constitution so that one may run for the presidency if they decide to enter the race for this coveted office. There are times when we try to take justice to the extreme, as if we can cure all social, financial, and mental illness. However, those who think that justice without punishment is politically correct are gravely mistaken. Our system is not a perfect system, but, despite all the imperfections of this wonderful democratic system, it is comforting to know there is justice.

One could say, after reminiscing about the past, that this country was at best unjust to the natives that inhabited it before Columbus came over and to the slaves that were brought here from Africa. You will always get a big "Amen" from me and from everyone who loves truth. But the Declaration of Independence is a document that breathes and fosters *justice* for all. When injustice occurs, everyone has a right to argue his or her case or be duly represented by legal counsel. If justice does not prevail, citizens have a right to protest with dignity and honor. As long as this flag of liberty and justice for all is hoisted up in this country, there will be liberty and justice for all. Some have to fight harder for it than others, but if we have the knowledge of our law and are willing to fight for what is rightfully ours, we may enjoy the fruit of liberty and justice for all.

CHAPTER 9
SINGING PRAISES FOR OUR COUNTRY

When an athlete wins a gold medal at the Olympics, the flag of the country that represents that athlete is raised above him or her, and that country's anthem is sung. What a proud moment for the triumphant persons standing on the platform, listening to their national anthem played over the loud speaker! The citizens and friends of that country burst out with accolades and applause while everyone else looks on. Mary Boibeaux of the Greater Grace Apostolic Church in Terryville, Connecticut, has this famous saying: "It is a poor frog that will not croak for its own pond." We should be able to sing about the country we live in. This does not mean we are worshiping the country. Only the Lord Jesus Christ should be worshipped. But, there is nothing wrong with loving, appreciating, and cherishing our country. America is a very good country. It is not perfect, but it is better than all the rest.

When I think of the Constitution, its Preamble, and all its Amendments, it gives me a warm sense of pride when I sing the songs that testify about the beauty and greatness of my country. Many songs have been written about this wonderful country of ours. My favorite is "Lift Every Voice and Sing." This is my favorite because I am a black American. This song speaks of the struggles Blacks had to go through and their will to persevere despite the obstacles thrown into their paths. This song does not condemn the oppressors; it puts hope in the offspring of the oppressed. Although I have to say my native land is America, I respect those that say Africa is their native land. I am an American, but will never deny the fact that my ancestors could have come from Africa. (I speak only for myself.) Many Blacks and people from other ethnic groups state that they are true to their native land but will not give one penny to help them in the time of crisis. I am an American!

"Lift Every Voice"
By James Weldon Johnson

Lift every voice and sing Till earth and heaven ring,
Ring with the harmonies of Liberty;
Let our rejoicing rise High as the listening skies,
Let it resound loud as the rolling sea.
Sing a song full of the faith that the dark past has taught us,
Sing a song full of the hope that the present has brought us,
Facing the rising sun of our new day begun
Let us march on till victory is won.
Stony the road we trod, Bitter the chastening rod,
Felt in the days when hope unborn had died;
Yet with a steady beat, Have not our weary feet
Come to the place for which our fathers sighed?
We have come over a way that with tears has been watered,
We have come, treading our path through the blood of the slaughtered,
Out from the gloomy past, Till now we stand at last
Where the white gleam of our bright star is cast.
God of our weary years, God of our silent tears,
Thou who has brought us thus far on the way;
Thou who has by Thy might Led us into the light,
Keep us forever in the path, we pray.
Lest our feet stray from the places, our God, where we met Thee,
Lest our hearts drunk with the wine of the world, we forget Thee;
Shadowed beneath Thy hand, May we forever stand.
True to our God, True to our native land.

The following song confirms our belief in God and thanks Him for giving us this land. Most songs today leave God out, but at the same time blame God for all the bad things that happen in this country. What an oxymoron! There will be a time in the future when songwriters and singers will regain their bravery to mention the name of the Lord. Jesus said if you are ashamed of Him, He would be ashamed of you. No true Christian should ever sign a contact that leaves God out of the songs they sing. The love of money is the root of all evil, and to leave God out of songs that should include Him is evil. What if He left you out?

"My Country Tis of Thee"
By Samuel F. Smith

My country, 'Tis of Thee, Sweet land of liberty,
Of Thee I sing;
Land where my fathers died, Land of the pilgrims' pride:

From every mountainside, Let freedom ring.

Our fathers' God, to Thee, Author of liberty,
To Thee we sing;
Long may our land be bright with freedom's holy light;
Protect us by Thy might, Great God, our King!

CHAPTER 10
In God We Trust

America is a country where religious freedom is enjoyed, but only if that religion is not geared toward human destruction. We hold English as the primary language to be spoken in this country. Likewise, we hold Christianity as the primary religion of the American people. The American government realizes they cannot set one intangible above another; therefore, they have not set Christianity as the official religion of the American people. However, the Founding Fathers and the hearts of the American people have made Christianity the official religion. Although Catholicism and the Church of England's religion were brought over to this country, Christianity was the only religion the early settlers of America practiced. Every other country that invested in the New World had Christian origins. They held that Jesus Christ was the Son of God, and tried to convince the natives of this truth. The hierarchy of Spain commanded Columbus not to enslave the natives, but to make them Christians. To reiterate, Columbus established the first colony with a principle of Christian theology. From that time forward the foundation was laid for this central belief.

We believe in the God of Moses. We believe in the Son of God, the Lord Jesus Christ. Our government opens its sessions with prayer to this God. When our schools used to do it, they were better because of it. Our currency has the phrase "In God We Trust" because we trust God. From our earliest existence to the prayers of the slaves to the wars to save the country and the world, and up to and beyond the recent attack on the Twin Towers on September 11, 2001, we continue to trust God. When we are faced with a serious attack on our people, as a whole we join together in a local church to pray that God will intervene and help us. When a child is lost, we pray that God will help us. When an adult is lost, we pray that God will help us. People who trusted in God started most of the hospitals in this country. When you are an inpatient at the hospital, you get a Bible to read because we trust God to help us.

God is not a religious title; He is a universal fact. Some people hate the fact that we use the phrase "In God We Trust." They hate our democratic why of life. They do not like the freedom we have. They know that the reason we have what we have is because we trust in God. No one can take that away from us, because it is branded far below our skin. It stains the soul until the soul becomes contagious. But, unlike contagions that kill, our trust in God spreads and produces life and that more abundantly. After 228 years, the serpent has uncovered its ugly head once again. But this time he allows for education and wealth, while subtly removing our trust in God from the entire population. If they can take the phrase "In God We Trust" from us, then they will proceed to take us. But they cannot because this is not just a phrase we use; this is our way of life.

If the atheists and their hypocritical anti-God friends have their way, they will prevent the word *God* from being spoken in public, in schools, in federal buildings, and even in churches. If they accomplish their evil purpose, in whom then can we trust? What moral law will uphold the federal law as a law to obey? Without the knowledge of the Most High God, the government will be the highest law. We know from the history of other countries what can happen when men rule solely over men. These atheists and their friends want to unravel the very fiber that has kept this country together. If they could, they would take our Constitution, the Preamble, and the Amendments and pour them in a secret melting pot. They would then take the good stuff and mix it with their own unstable, philosophical, humanistic ways. Then they would wait for the garbage to rise to the top. Then they would take a big dipper to remove the residue they consider garbage. After they stirred around for a while only to realize that the garbage was their own philosophy, they would change what they found, then present the good stuff to the people as garbage so that everyone could form their own opinion. This is exactly what happened recently in Massachusetts when they made it possible for people of the same sex to marry. When they could not find the garbage of the law, they made the truth look like garbage and fed it to the constituents. Now they have sperm trying to marry sperm and egg trying to marry egg. Regardless of the garbage that has been presented as law, the law of God will never change. It is "In God We Trust."

BLACK AFRICANS THAT REFUSED TO BE SLAVES

Many black and white Americans believed that every slave that was brought and sold to this country was completely submissive with fear and trembling. The reality was quite to the contrary. They were not as docile as their masters thought. Prior to the signing of the Emancipation Proclamation Act on January 1, 1863, slaves fought to the death to be free from the brutal system of American slavery. Even though the practice of killing slaves, cutting their limbs off, and killing family members in front of entire groups, caused the majority of slaves to reconsider their attempt to be free, these cruel tactics did not stop thousands from seeking their God-given rights of life and liberty. Exodus 21:20-21 states, "And if a man beats his male or female servant with a rod, so that he dies under his hand, he shall surely be punished. Notwithstanding, if he remains alive a day or two, he shall not be punished, for he is his property." God punished former slave masters and friends for their ill treatment of the black African slaves. God is still punishing evil slave masters through their descendents. One of the primary ways God is punishing the evil slave master is by remembrance. Every time the name of an evil former slave owner is mentioned, the descendents are forced to bear the shame of their remembrance. I can only hope that those descendents can move forward so that this evil legacy is not part of their future. On the other hand, people like George Washington, Benjamin Franklin, and Thomas Jefferson were very good to their slaves. The descendents of these few fine men have memories they can feel proud of. Blacks and white civil rights proponents may ask, how can one be proud of slave owners? Keep in mind that slaves had to be here in America. Therefore, I thank God for the people who had loving and righteous hearts and were good to their slaves.

Below is a list of chronological order that history unveils to show that America had many problems trying to keep the black Africans enslaved.

Major revolts and escapes:

1663—First serious slave conspiracy in Colonial America, September 13th. Servant betrayed plot of White servants and Negro slaves in Gloucester County, Virginia.

1712—Slave revolt, New York, April 7th. Nine Whites killed; twenty-one slaves executed.

1730—Slave conspiracy discovered in Norfolk and Princess Anne counties, Virginia.

1739—Slave revolt, Stono, South Carolina, September 9th. Twenty-five Whites killed before insurrection was put down.

1741—Series of suspicious fires and reports of slave conspiracy led to general hysteria in New York City in March and April. Thirty-one slaves and five Whites executed.

1773—Massachusetts slaves petitioned legislature for freedom, January 6th. There is a record of eight petitions during the Revolutionary War period.

1800—Gabriel Prosser plotted and was betrayed. Storm forced suspension of attack on Richmond, Virginia, by Prosser and some one thousand slaves, August 30th. His conspiracy was betrayed by two slaves. Prosser and fifteen of his followers were hanged on October 7th.

1811—Louisiana slaves revolted in two parishes about thirty-five miles from New Orleans, January 8-10. Revolt suppressed by U. S. troops. This is believed to be the largest slave revolt in the United States.

1816—Three hundred fugitive slaves and about twenty Indian allies held Fort Blount on Apalachicola Bay, Florida, for several days before it was attacked by U. S. Troops.

1822—Denmark Vesey plotted and was betrayed. "House slave" betrayed Denmark Vesey conspiracy, May 30th. Vesey conspiracy, one of the most elaborate slave plots on record, involved thousands of Negroes in Charleston, South Carolina, and vicinity. Authorities arrested 131 Negroes and four whites. Thirty-seven were hanged. Vesey and five of his aides hanged at Blake's Landing, Charleston, South Carolina, July 2nd.

1829—Race riot, Cincinnati, Ohio, August 10th. More than one thousand Negroes left the city for Canada.

1831—Nat Turner revolt, Southampton County, Virginia, August 21st-22nd. Some sixty Whites were killed. Nat Turner was not captured until October 30th. Nat Turner was hanged, Jerusalem, Virginia, November 11th.

1838—Frederick Douglass escaped from slavery in Baltimore, September 3rd.

1839—*Amistad* mutiny led by Joseph Cinquez, captured. After trial in Connecticut, returned to Africa.

1841—Slave revolt on slave trader *Creole* which was en route from Hampton, Virginia, to New Orleans, Louisiana, November 7th. Slaves overpowered crew and sailed vessel to Bahamas where they were granted asylum and freedom.

1848—Ellen Craft impersonated a slaveholder; her husband William Craft acted as her servant in one of the most dramatic slave escapes. She was the daughter of a white slave owner in Macon, Georgia. While she and her husband were trailing, she would tell people that she was on her way to Philadelphia to get medical supplies. She arrived there on December 25, 1848.

1849—Harriet Tubman escaped from slavery in Maryland, summer. She returned to the South nineteen times and brought out more than three hundred slaves.

1851—Negro abolitionist crashed into courtroom in Boston and rescued a fugitive slave, February 15th. Negroes dispersed group of slave catchers September 11th in Christiana, Pennsylvania, conflict. One White man was killed, another wounded. Negro and White abolitionists smashed into courtroom in Syracuse, New York, and rescued a fugitive slave October 1st.[36]

CHAPTER 11
THE SLAVES HAD TO BE SET FREE

On June 28, 1776, Thomas Jefferson presented his first draft of the Declaration of Independence to the Continental Congress, which they then debated. The important revision excised his pointed attack on the slave trade, in which the Virginia slaveholder had charged the King of England with having "waged cruel war against human nature itself, violating its most sacred rights of life and liberty in the persons of a distant people who never offended him, captivating and carrying them into slavery." The most important revision excised Jefferson's pointed attack on "[incurring] miserable death in their transportation hither, this piratical warfare, [and] the opprobrium of infidel powers [by] the Christian King of Great Britain."

Because slavery was so profitable to the southern delegates, they objected to Jefferson's attack, and persuaded some northern delegates to have his draft removed. If the southerners' objections to the first draft had been defeated, slavery would have been abolished more than a hundred years before President Lincoln freed the slaves and saved the Union. The descendents of the black African slaves would have been one hundred years more advanced than what they were. So, enslavement was not about hatred; it was about economic opportunity and wealth. The ex-slaves became hated when the ex-masters lost control over their ability to have people work without wages.

As president of the Pennsylvania Society for Promoting the Abolition of Slavery, Benjamin Franklin signed a petition to Congress on February 12, 1790, for immediate abolishment of slavery. Six weeks later, in his most brilliant manner, Franklin parodied the attack on the petition made by James Jackson (1757-1806) of Georgia, taking off Jackson's quotations of Scripture with pretended texts from the Koran cited by a member of the Divan of Algiers in opposition to a petition asking for the prohibition of holding Christians in slavery. Franklin wrote to the Senate and the House of Representative of the United States on February 3, 1790, opposing slavery. Franklin did not speak out against slavery until his later years. Soon after he wrote this letter he passed away on April 17, 1790.[37] But his stand was strong and compelling. Many members from the Society continued their fight for the abolishment of slavery as a result Franklin's involvement.

The question may be asked, why did Franklin, who had slaves and advertised the trading of slaves in his newspaper, wait so long before fighting for the abolishment of slavery in America? Not to justify Benjamin Franklin or anyone that held the black Africans in slavery, but owning slaves was a way of life. Because of his belief in God, Franklin corrected this flaw by releasing all of his slaves and fighting for the release of others. I graciously honor his name for eventually having the courage to recognize that his own actions were wrong. Because of God's plan for these people to participate in the prosperity of this great country, it would have been impossible for some black Africans not to be enslaved. Therefore, Franklin's ownership of black Africans at that time was a blessing for them.

ANTISLAVERY MOVEMENT

Underneath the concrete thinking of man is an abstract truth that can only be understood by those who are willing to accept that truth without the approval of the majority. When truth is accepted, it can be proclaimed even by the simplest mind. The truth is that the slaves had to be set free in America. Even if slavery continued to exist in other parts of the world, slavery had to be abolished in America. Whether it was one year after the black Africans arrived, or two hundred years after they arrived, slavery had to be abolished.

America was established to offer both religious and political freedom. Freedom was not just a document; it was God's gift to humanity when He created us in His own image. In the church culture we call *freedom* a "spirit"; the very essence of what inspires us. Those who believed in this spirit of freedom worked hard to free the slaves. Slavery could not exist where the spirit of freedom prevailed. Freedom worked against slavery, and slavery was the antithesis of freedom. The spirit of freedom was the foundation of our existence. All that touched American soil must be free. If not, then wars and killing would permeate the days, months, and years until freedom was granted. As I stated earlier, I believe that the black Africans came as slaves to this country by divine will. I stand with a few others without apology or shame to declare this truth. After reading the Bible and accepting it as the one true guide for man, it would be impossible for me not to see the hand of God working out His purpose for some of the black Africans and their descendents (especially me).

Step by step, God orchestrated His plan. The Quakers began their Criticism in 1617. In France, the Society of the Friends of the Blacks (Societe des Amis Noirs) was founded in 1788. By the late eighteenth century, moral disapproval of slavery was widespread (led by evangelicals), and antislavery reformers gained a number of seemingly easy victories. In Britain, Granville Sharp, working alone, secured a decision in the Somersett case (1772) that West Indian planters could not hold slaves in England, since slavery was contrary to English law. In America, the leading figures of the revolutionary period that condemned slavery were men such as Thomas Jefferson and Benjamin Franklin. Between 1777 and 1804, all the states north of Maryland abolished it. Others gradually phased it out.

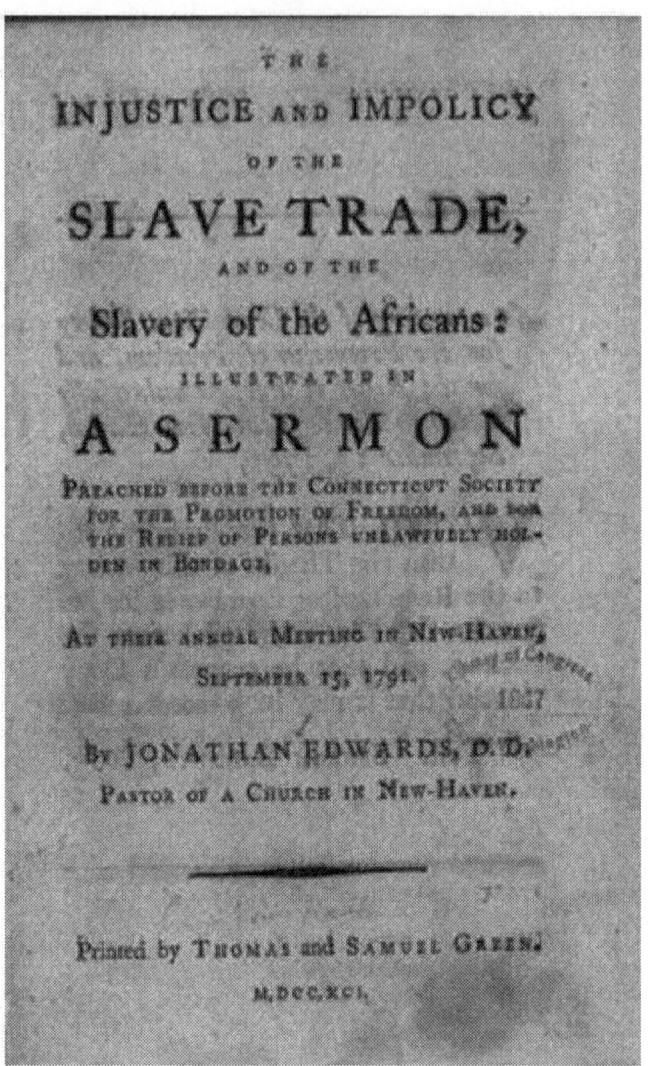

*Jonathan Edwards, Jr. (1745-1801) was, like his more
famous father, a Congregationalist minister. He served at
the White Haven Church in New Haven, Connecticut, and
later became president of Union College in Schenectady,
New York. In this sermon, Edwards presented forceful
arguments against ten common proslavery positions. One
of the earliest antislavery publications in the Library of
Congress collections, the sermon demonstrates the existence
of strong antislavery feeling in the early days of the republic.*

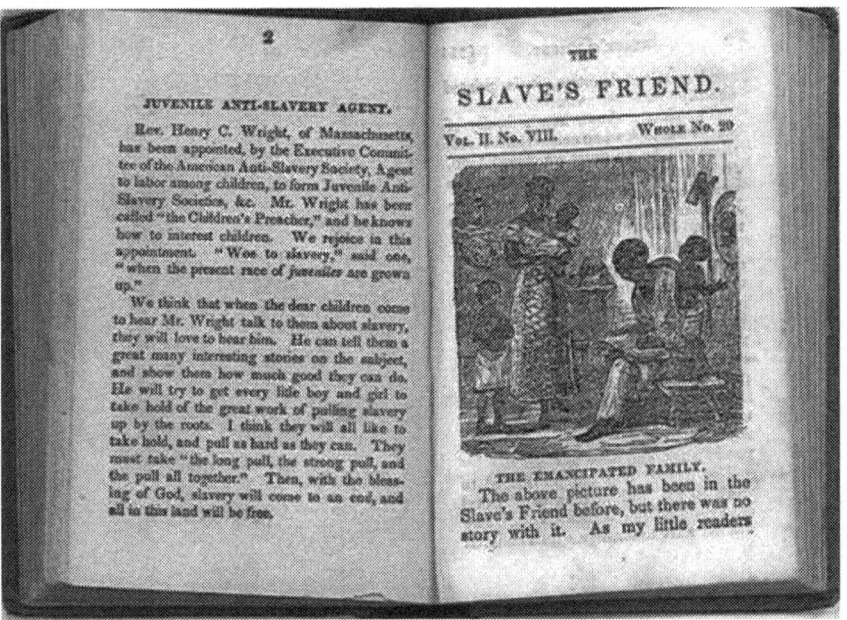

The American Antislavery Society produced The Slave's
Friend, *a monthly pamphlet of abolitionist poems, songs,
and stories for children. In its pages, young readers were
encouraged to collect money for the antislavery cause.
Here a picture of the coffle-yoke used to chain groups of
slaves together illustrates a dialogue about the horrors
of slavery between a girl named Ellen and her father,
Mr. Murray. A shocked Ellen concluded, "I will never
boast of our liberty while there is a slave in this land."*

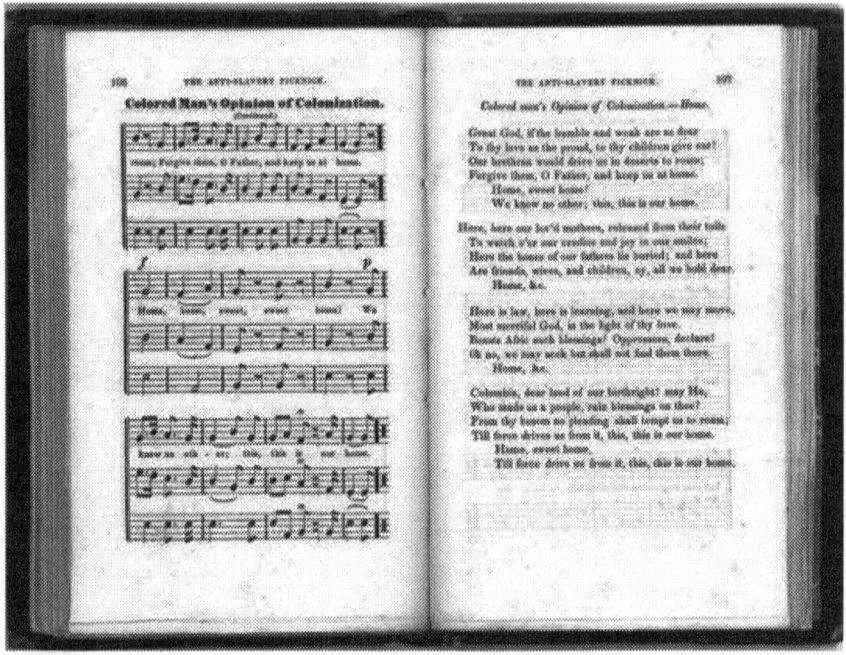

Anti-colonization sentiment was common in abolitionist publications such as The Antislavery Picknick, a collection of speeches, poems, dialogues, and songs intended for use in schools and antislavery meetings. A song called the "Colored Man's Opinion of Colonization" denounced plans to transport free Blacks out of the United States. Many African Americans opposed colonization, and, in 1831, a convention of free Blacks meeting in New York asserted, "This is our home, and this is our country. Beneath its sod lie the bones of our fathers; for it some of them fought, bled, and died. Here we were born, and here we will die."

In 1787 the Abolition Society, consisting mostly of Quakers, was formed. Under William Wilberforce and Thomas Clarkson, the slave trade to British colonies was finally abolished in 1807. The antislavery groups hoped that after the slave trade had ended, slavery itself would gradually go away, but this did not happen. Because slavery did not go away, a group of men started a revolution to abolish slavery in America forever. Among these were Thomas Fewell Buxton, 1823 (Anti Slavery Society), William Lloyd Garrison, 1831 (editor of the *Liberator* and founder of the American Society, 1832), and the most prominent of the three was Theodore Dwight Weld, 1803-1895 (preacher—Seventy Apostles).

Theodore D. Weld wrote *American Slavery as It Is: Testimony of a Thousand Witnesses*. This lengthy, in-depth argument defined American slavery as a "cancer to the human race." Weld spelled out the sin of slavery by listing numerous examples of how individual slaves were mistreated. One of the most gruesome examples was an account of a person having the head of a slave inside his coat. Anyone who reads these accounts will feel anger, wrath, guilt, condemnation, or even hatred. These revelations sent a message to all men that slavery had to be abolished even if it cost lives.[38]

Before the start of Civil War, the spirit of freedom sat so heavily on those who believed it was wrong for slaveholders to treat human beings so inhumanely that they could no longer tolerate slavery in the United States of America. What many black Americans do not know and cannot accept is that many white Americans engaged in the fight to free the slaves. Teachers of Black History focus only on the success of the Blacks and omit the contribution of the Whites who gave their lives for the cause of freedom for all men. Truth includes all of history, whether it praises us or dishonors us. Truth does not tell only one side of the story. This is why the Holy Bible is so important to us; it tells the entire story.

JOHN BROWN, A BROTHER FOR FREEDOM

John Brown (1800-1859) was a truly great American. His story must be told in this book. Every black and white American must know John Brown's story. When he said, "Bury me with my brothers," he was referring to Black slaves.

Harboring a fury that was fueled by profound religious devotion, John Brown carried his hatred of slavery into action, creating a legacy of bloodshed and violence that remains at once inspiring and appalling.

Born in Torrington, Connecticut, in 1800 into a deeply religious family, Brown spent much of his childhood in the antislavery stronghold of Ohio. Setting out in life as a businessman, he went from mild success to repeated failure, and from 1825 to 1855 he moved his large family ten times, shifting his occupation from tanner to shepherd to farmer and working at whatever odd jobs he could find. Always a committed abolitionist, during these years he offered his homes as way-stops on the Underground Railroad and insisted that his churches admit African Americans as full members of their congregations.

In 1855 Brown followed five of his sons to Kansas when they appealed to him for help in fighting off the Missouri border ruffians who were gathering there to force slavery on the citizens of the territory. Brown arrived with a wagonload of weapons and the conviction that all free soil in Kansas stood in mortal peril. In 1856 Brown felt compelled to take action. During the night of May 24th, he led a group that methodically killed five pro-slavery settlers living along Pottawatomie Creek, dragging the men out of their cabins and butchering them with swords.

This massacre shocked even Brown's fellow abolitionists and led to a string of violent deaths that gave rise to the name "Bleeding Kansas." Brown successfully fought off all attempts to apprehend him and maintained publicly that his acts were not only justified, but were also directly ordered by God. Finally, in October, he left Kansas for a tour through the Northeast, where he was acclaimed for his militant opposition to slavery. But by this time Brown had formulated an even more militant plan: he would incite a massive slave insurrection and thereby destroy the hated institution once and for all. To provide the funding for this ambitious undertaking, he turned to wealthy abolitionists who had grown frustrated by the failure of peaceful means and shared his view that it was time to wage war.

After returning to Kansas briefly in 1858 where he led a raiding party into Missouri, which liberated eleven slaves, Brown moved in early 1859 to a rented farm near Harpers Ferry, Virginia, site of a federal arsenal with which Brown planned to arm the slaves he would inspire to rebellion. In October, he led twenty-one followers in a raid on Harpers Ferry and quickly occupied the federal arsenal but was just as quickly trapped there by troops under the command of Robert E. Lee. The next morning Lee's forces overran Brown's band of raiders, killing half of them, including two of Brown's sons.

Brown's ensuing trial for treason gave him the opportunity to vigorously condemn slavery and to again defend his actions as ordained by God. Before his hanging in December, popular support poured out of the North. The white South, however, was only more deeply convinced that remaining in the Union meant the end of slavery. Yet both sides could agree that, as he had in Kansas, John Brown had sharpened the issue dividing them into a weapon that would not be sheathed until it had drawn blood.

THE START OF THE CIVIL WAR

Fueled by John Brown's death two years past, America found itself divided. The Union that had won independence from British rule found itself struggling to continue as one. The spirit of freedom and the spirit of slavery met in the center of the ring. Neither one would declare the other as champion of the Union. When they went into their individual corners and viewed their fans for the last time before returning to the center of the ring to do battle, they realized that only one of them would walk out alive. As they squared off, freedom threw the first punch. It caught slavery right on the chin. Slavery's knees buckled. His supporters, fans, and friends realized that freedom fought with every intention of killing him. Like many people who jump on bandwagons, some proponents of slavery saw that their star did not have a chance and jumped to the other side. Friends of slavery and freedom that had tolerated each other became enemies when they saw that freedom was determined to win the fight. Slavery became weak, but when he heard cheers from his fans, he refused to submit. When his proponents saw his buoyancy, they cheered louder in the hope that slavery would win. But slavery was no match for freedom. Freedom had many more and stronger supporters on his side. Freedom knew that it was destined to win and grew stronger and more determined because of this knowledge. The crowd of supporters for both sides grew so hostile they split the country.

Finally in 1861 the Civil War broke out in the United States of America. The southern states broke away from the Union and formed the Confederate State of America. The northern states continued with the name Union and vowed to help the spirit of freedom free the black African slaves. The war started on April 12, 1861, when Confederate troops fired on Fort Sumter, a U. S. military post in Charleston, South Carolina.

This war took more American lives than any other war in America's history. It so divided the people of the United States that in some families brothers fought against brothers. The bloodshed of the war was so terrible that it left a heritage of grief and bitterness. Grief and bitterness would die out in later generations, but slavery had to be abolished right then and there. White men, black men, white women, black women, and children of both groups died to help the cause of freedom.

The Civil War lasted almost four years from the day it started. On April 9, 1865, Confederate General Robert E. Lee surrendered his army to Union General Ulysses S. Grant at Appomattox Court

House, a small Virginia settlement. The other Confederate forces gave up soon after. Julia Howe saw as it were angels fighting for the cause of freedom and penned the following song. Slavery was defeated, because freedom had seen the end from the beginning and would not give up. Freedom was the victor.

"BATTLE HYMN OF THE REPUBLIC,"
SECOND VERSION
By Julia Howe

Mine eyes have seen the glory of the coming of the Lord,
He is trampling out the vintage where
    the grapes of wrath are stored,
He has loosed the fateful lightning of his terrible swift sword,
His truth is marching on.

CHORUS
Glory, Glory Hallelujah, Glory, Glory Hallelujah,
Glory, Glory Hallelujah, His truth is marching on.

He has sounded forth the trumpet that
    shall never call retreat,
He is sifting out the hearts of men before His judgment seat.
Be swift my soul to answer him, be jubilant my feet,
Our God is marching on.
In the beauty of the lilies Christ was born across the sea,
With a glory in his bosom, That transfigures you and me,
As He died to make men Holy, let us die to make men free,
His truth is marching on.

In 1863 a new era dawned for the black African slaves: freedom. Unconditionally, they became American citizens. The great news of freedom was heralded in many forms, but it did not matter until the federal government proclaimed it in writing.

President Abraham Lincoln signed into law the emancipation of all American black African slaves.

EMANCIPATION PROCLAMATION: JANUARY 1, 1863

Whereas, on the twenty-second day of September, in the year of our Lord one thousand eight hundred and sixty-two, a proclamation was issued by the president of the United States, containing, among other things, the following, to wit:

That on the first day of January, in the year of our Lord one thousand eight hundred and sixty-three, all persons held as slaves within any State or designated part of a State, the people whereof shall then be in rebellion against the United States, shall be then, thenceforward, and forever free; and the Executive Government of the United States, including the military and naval authority thereof, will recognize and maintain the freedom of such persons, and will do no act or acts to repress such persons, or any of them, in any efforts they may make for their actual freedom.

That the Executive will, on the first day of January aforesaid, by proclamation, designate the States and parts of States, if any, in which the people thereof, respectively, shall then be in rebellion against the United States; and the fact that any State, or the people thereof, shall on that day be, in good faith, represented in the Congress of the United States by members chosen thereto at elections wherein a majority of the qualified voters of such State shall have participated, shall, in the absence of strong countervailing testimony, be deemed conclusive evidence that such State, and the people thereof, are not then in rebellion against the United States.

Now, therefore I, Abraham Lincoln, president of the United States, by virtue of the power in me vested as Commander-in-Chief, of the Army and Navy of the United States in time of actual armed rebellion against the authority and government of the United States, and as a fit and necessary war measure for suppressing said rebellion, do, on this first day of January, in the year of our Lord one thousand eight hundred and sixty-three, and in accordance with my purpose so to do publicly proclaimed for the full period of one hundred days, from the day first above mentioned, order and designate as the States and parts of States wherein the people thereof respectively, are this day in rebellion against the United States, the following, to wit:

Arkansas, Texas, Louisiana, (except the Parishes of St. Bernard, Plaquemines, Jefferson, St. John, St. Charles, St. James Ascension, Assumption, Terrebonne, Lafourche, St. Mary, St. Martin, and Orleans, including the City of New Orleans) Mississippi, Alabama, Florida, Georgia, South Carolina, North Carolina, and Virginia, (except the forty-eight counties designated as West Virginia, and also the counties of Berkley, Accomac, Northampton, Elizabeth City, York, Princess Ann, and Norfolk, including the cities of Norfolk and Portsmouth), and which excepted parts, are for the present, left precisely as if this proclamation were not issued.

And by virtue of the power, and for the purpose aforesaid, I do order and declare that all persons held as slaves within said designated States, and parts of States, are, and henceforward shall be free; and that the Executive government of the United States, including the military and naval authorities thereof, will recognize and maintain the freedom of said persons.

And I hereby enjoin upon the people so declared to be free to abstain from all violence, unless in necessary self-defense; and I recommend to them that, in all cases when allowed, they labor faithfully for reasonable wages.

And I further declare and make known, that such persons of suitable condition, will be received into the armed service of the United States to garrison forts, positions, stations, and other places, and to man vessels of all sorts in said service.

And upon this act, sincerely believed to be an act of justice, warranted by the Constitution, upon military necessity, I invoke the considerate judgment of mankind, and the gracious favor of Almighty God.

In witness whereof, I have hereunto set my hand and caused the seal of the United States to be affixed.

Done at the City of Washington, this first day of January, in the year of our Lord one thousand eight hundred and sixty three, and of the Independence of the United States of America the eighty-seventh.

By the President: ABRAHAM LINCOLN
WILLIAM H. SEWARD, Secretary of State.[39]

AMENDMENT XIII

Passed by Congress January 31, 1865. Ratified December 6, 1865.

Note: A portion of Article IV, section 2, of the Constitution was superseded by the 13th amendment.

Section 1.

Neither slavery nor involuntary servitude, except as a punishment for crime whereof the party shall have been duly convicted, shall exist within the United States, or any place subject to their jurisdiction.

Section 2.

Congress shall have power to enforce this article by appropriate legislation.

AMENDMENT XIV

Passed by Congress June 13, 1866. Ratified July 9, 1868.

Note: Article I, section 2, of the Constitution was modified by section 2 of the 14th amendment.

Section 1.

All persons born or naturalized in the United States, and subject to the jurisdiction thereof, are citizens of the United States and of the State wherein they reside. No State shall make or enforce any law, which shall abridge the privileges or immunities of citizens of the United States; nor shall any State deprive any person of life, liberty, or property, without due process of law; nor deny to any person within its jurisdiction the equal protection of the laws.

Section 2.

Representatives shall be apportioned among the several States according to their respective numbers, counting the whole number of persons in each State, excluding Indians not taxed. But when the right to vote at any election for the choice of electors for president and vice president of the United States, Representatives in Congress, the Executive and Judicial officers of a State, or the members of the Legislature thereof, is denied to any of the male inhabitants of such State, being twenty-one years of age, * and citizens of the United States, or in any way abridged, except for participation in rebellion, or other crime, the basis of representation therein shall be reduced in the proportion which the number of such male citizens shall bear to the whole number of male citizens twenty-one years of age in such State.

Section 3.

No person shall be a Senator or Representative in Congress, or elector of president and vice president, or hold any office, civil or military, under the United States, or under any State, who, having previously taken an oath, as a member of Congress, or as an officer of the United States, or as a member of any State legislature, or as an executive or judicial officer of any State, to support the Constitution of the United States, shall have engaged in insurrection or rebellion against the same, or given aid or comfort to the enemies thereof. But Congress may by a vote of two-thirds of each House, remove such disability.

Section 4.

The validity of the public debt of the United States, authorized by law, including debts incurred for payment of pensions and bounties for services in suppressing insurrection or rebellion, shall not be questioned. But neither the United States nor any State shall assume or pay any debt or obligation incurred in aid of insurrection or rebellion against the United States, or any claim for the loss or emancipation of any slave; but all such debts, obligations and claims shall be held illegal and void.

Section 5.

The Congress shall have the power to enforce, by appropriate legislation, the provisions of this article.

*Changed by section 1 of the 26th amendment.

AMENDMENT XV

Passed by Congress February 26, 1869. Ratified February 3, 1870.

Section 1.

The right of citizens of the United States to vote shall not be denied or abridged by the United States or by any State on account of race, color, or previous condition of servitude.

Section 2.

The Congress shall have the power to enforce this article by appropriate legislation.

*Emancipation of the slaves, proclaimed on the
22nd September 1862, by Abraham Lincoln,
President of the United States of America.
Lithograph by J. Waeshle.*[40]

The (Fort) Monroe Doctrine

On May 27, 1861, Benjamin Butler, commander of the Union army in Virginia and North Carolina, decreed that slaves who fled to Union lines were legitimate "contraband of war" and were not subject to being returned to their Confederate owners. The declaration precipitated scores of escapes to Union lines around Fortress Monroe, Butler's headquarters in Virginia. In this crudely drawn caricature, a slave stands before the Union fort taunting his plantation master. The planter (right) waves his whip and cries, "Come back, you black rascal." The slave replies, "Can't come back nohow massa. Dis chile's contraban." Hordes of other slaves are seen leaving the fields and heading toward the fort.[41]

CHAPTER 12
New Citizens

After the Civil War (1861-1865) over the question of slavery, three Amendments to the U. S. Constitution significantly altered the scope and nature of American democracy. Ratified in 1865, the Thirteenth Amendment abolished slavery forever. The fourteenth, ratified in 1868, declared that all persons born or naturalized in the United States were citizens of the country and of the state in which they resided, and that their rights to life, liberty, property, and the equal protection of the laws were to be enforced by the federal government. Ratified in 1870, the Fifteenth Amendment prohibited federal or state governments from discriminating against potential voters because of race, color, or previous condition of servitude.

Because the crucial word *sex* was left off this anti-discrimination list, women continued to be barred from the polls. However, the extension of suffrage to include former slaves gave new life to the long-simmering campaign for women's right to vote. This battle was finally won in 1920, when the Nineteenth Amendment guaranteed that voting could not be denied "on account of sex."

Ironically, at this point the situation was reversed. Women could now vote, but many black Americans could not. Beginning in the 1890s, southern Whites had systematically removed Blacks from electoral politics through voting regulations such as the "grandfather clause" (which required literacy tests for all citizens whose ancestors had not been voters before 1868), the imposition of poll taxes, and, too often, physical intimidation. This disfranchisement continued well into the twentieth century. The Civil Rights Movement, which began in the 1950s, resulted in the Voting Rights Act of 1965, a federal law that outlawed unfair electoral procedures and required that the Department of Justice supervise southern elections. The Twenty-fourth Amendment, ratified in 1964, abolished the imposition of a poll tax as a qualification for voting, eliminating one of the few remaining ways that states could try to reduce voting by black Americans and poor white people.

Regardless of the history in this country concerning the mistreatment of Indians and black African Americans, this is our home. We were born in America and are therefore citizens.

We are not black Americans, African Americans, or colored Americans, but simply Americans. Logically and politically, there is a danger in the true descendents of American slaves being called African Americans. Past ideologies among the majority do not die easily. They have to be killed by stabbing the vicious ideological giant in the heart, and then they must cut off its head.

We are not a Pilgrims. Pilgrims are people who pass through a certain place. They do not intend to purchase anything other than the necessities of life. They do not care about citizenship, so they do not wish to be called by the name of the local dwellers. I am not a pilgrim in America; I am a local. To allow the majority to think you are not a pure citizen is to deprive yourself of the same freedom enjoyed by them. The fallacy that people are on your side or in your corner because they come to your parties, watch you perform in athletic events, or cheer when you do something wonderful, will become evident when you try to become equal with them. Only Americans can truly get the benefits of America. Americans will pat strangers on the back and say good job, but they are not one of us. So, what if the others citizens of this country still consider themselves part of the nations from which their ancestors came? This is implied by the following designations: Italian Americans, Polish Americans, Greek Americans, Irish Americans, and African Americans. The one thing black Americans must always understand is that the color of their skin puts them in a category behind everyone else in America. The ideological view of black Americans is as entertainers, not leaders. Entertainers make you laugh and possibly help remove some of life's problems for the moment. After the show, you are put back in the cage until the next event. Like Pinocchio, you are not a real boy. Thankfully, not everyone in the majority thinks this way. After a white interviewer stated he was not like most Whites because he believed in giving Coloreds equal rights but that he still believed in separate schools, the former slave replied, "You still have the disease, baby. You can't give me rights. God gave me my rights."[42] Discrimination is a disease that still affects some. Only Christ and time will be able to heal people. During the Columbine crisis we had a meeting at one of the local high schools. We were discussing Connecticut's Choice Program, which allows students from one district to attend schools in other districts. At the end of what I would call a successful meeting, one of the dear white women made one of the most humiliating statements of her life. She said, "I hope we are not participating in the program, because I am afraid that inner city kids could come in and start problems in our school." Before I could say anything, another white woman said to her, "Did you not hear what was said in the meeting? Did you see that it was our white kids that killed these children? Are you so blind that you can't see it wasn't kids from the inner city that caused these problems?" The dear woman who had made the first statement just sat and looked as if to say, how dare you white people turn on me? I'm one of you.

No! You are not one of us. If you do not do the right thing, you are not one of us. We do not have color; we have character. Color should never take precedence over character.

Black Americans should refuse to be called anything but Americans. The only exception to this would be designating

139

oneself by race to the government during a census. Because of the many people in one nation, I feel that it is okay to be listed as a black American or an African American or an Irish American or a Polish American or an Italian American or an Asian American or any other group. We are not citizens of any other country. We are citizens of this country. Anything other than citizenship is subtly considered slavery. Therefore, we should act according to good citizenship and demand all the freedom that is rightfully ours as citizens.

CHAPTER 13
THE MONUMENTAL
ENCOURAGEMENT

THE STATUE OF LIBERTY (LADY LIBERTY)

America probably could not have won its freedom from the British during the American Revolution without the help of the French. France provided arms, ships, money, and men to the American Colonies. Some Frenchmen—most notably the Marquis de Lafayette, a close friend of George Washington—even became high-ranking officers in the American army. It was an alliance of respect and friendship the French would not forget.

In 1776 America won it independence from Britain, almost one hundred ten years later France embodied its respect and friendship through three noble Frenchmen: Frederic Auguste Bartholdi, Edouard de Laboulaye, and Count Fredinand de Lesseps. The most memorable was Bartholdi for his work, the Statue of Liberty.

Frederic Auguste Bartholdi was born into a well-to-do middle-class family in Colmar, France, on August 2, 1834. Bartholdi's father, a civil servant and prosperous landowner, died when he was only two years old, so his stern, possessive mother, Charlotte, raised him.

Bartholdi began his career as a painter, but it was as a sculptor that he expressed his true spirit and gained his greatest fame. His first commission for a public monument came to him at the young age of eighteen. It was for a statue of one of Colmar's native sons, General Jean Rapp, one of Napoleon Bonaparte's generals. Even at eighteen, Bartholdi loved bigness. The statue of the general was twelve feet tall and was removed from Bartholdi's studio with only one inch to spare. The statue established his reputation as a sculptor of note and led to commissions for similar oversized patriotic works.

Bartholdi, a man of his time, was not alone in his passion for art on a grand scale. During the nineteenth century, large-scale public monuments were an especially popular art form. It was an age of ostentation, largely inspired by classical Greek and Roman civilizations. Most monuments reflected either the dress or architecture of these ancient times, so the artistic style of the nineteenth century came to be known as neoclassical. However, a trip to Egypt shifted Bartholdi's artistic perspective from simply grand to colossal. The overwhelming size and mysterious majesty of the Pyramids and the Sphinx were awesome to the enthusiastic young Bartholdi. He wrote, "Their kindly and impassive glance seems to ignore the present and to be fixed upon an unlimited future." Notice that he was in Egypt when he acquired these impressions. The serenity of the people never left him. He imposed this same serenity on the face and grace of the Statue of Liberty.

While visiting Egypt, Bartholdi met a fellow Frenchman by the name of Count Ferdinand-Marie de Lesseps with ideas as big as his own and who was to become his friend for life. Count de Lesseps dreamed of piercing the desert with a canal that would run from the Mediterranean Sea to the Red Sea. While others first laughed at de Lesseps, Bartholdi was inspired by the magnitude of the idea. As a sculptor, he envisioned a giant lighthouse standing at the entrance to de Lesseps's canal. It would be patterned after the Roman goddess Libertas, and twice the size of the Sphinx.

Throughout the Civil War, some French imperials had sought to aid the Confederacy. Another one of Bartholdi's associates in the statue project, De Laboulaye, wrote, "Until a new sort of politics was lately found for us, it was accepted on both sides of the ocean as a virtual article of faith that America and France are sisters. . . . We claim that France never fights for an interest, only for an ideal. I accept this proud device and ask: If we aid the South, what ideal shall we be defending?"

Shortly after the close of the American Civil War and just after the assassination of President Lincoln, the people of France took up a collection limited to two cents per donor. Along with this collection, they designed a gold medal, which they sent to the president's widow. The message from the people read, "Tell Mrs. Lincoln that in this little box is the heart of France." The medal bore the words in French: "Dedicated by French democracy to Lincoln, twice-elected president of the United States—honest Lincoln who abolished slavery, reestablished the union, and saved the Republic, without veiling the Statue of Liberty."

In 1865, De Laboulaye invited some prominent guests to dinner. One of them was a young sculptor, Frederic Auguste Bartholdi. De Laboulaye made a point to the distinguished guest that bonds between France and the United States were lasting ones. He suggested that a monument be built to commemorate the achieving of America's independence and that it should be constructed jointly by both countries.

Years later after serving in the French Army, the young sculptor Bartholdi remembered the conversation with De Laboulaye and thought of making America his home because his native home had been destroyed. With the ideal of a monument and the thought of America as his home, he revisited De Laboulaye at Versailles. De Laboulaye again started his sentiments for America and wish that a celebration for the one hundred years of her independence could be done by display. He suggested that Bartholdi go to America, study the situation, and discuss with friends there the possibility that they work together on a monument to commemorate the long friendship of France and the United States. Inspired, Bartholdi left for the United States, carrying letters of introduction from the eminent men with whom the project had been discussed at Versailles.

Bartholdi wrote years later, "Laboulaye said to me go see that country. Propose to our friends over there to make with us a monument, a common work, in remembrance of the ancient friendship of France and the United States. If ... you find a plan that will excite public enthusiasm, we are convinced that it will be successful on both continents, and we will do a work that will have far-reaching moral effect. I responded, I will try to glorify the Republic and Liberty over there, in the hope that someday I will find it again here."

In 1867 with de Lesseps's ideal, the Suez Canal, nearing completion, Bartholdi drew up plans for his statue. It was to be in the form of a robed female Egyptian peasant, a falaha, with light beaming out from both a headband and a torch thrust dramatically upward into the skies. Many people believed Charlotte Bartholdi (1801-1891) was the model for the statue. Others thought it was based on her son's early drawings for a never-commissioned statue in Egypt. For some, the sculptor's true inspiration for his masterpiece remains a mystery. But the statue that he sculptured for the American people was not the composition of a French woman. It resembled an Egyptian woman by the fact that her dress and facial structure was made in the image of an ancient Egyptian woman. A careful look at the ancient Egyptian people would lead one to believe that the features of the statue resemble more closely an Egyptian woman than a French woman. Therefore, the Lady's resemblance to the features of black slaves should dispel any mystery about whom the statue resembles.

Bartholdi's plan was accepted, and a Franco-American Union was formed in 1875. But prior to this, he had already made several model statues. In 1877 Richard Morris Hunt was selected by the

American Committee to design the pedestal, for which he was paid $1,000. General Charles P. Stone was the chief engineer in charge of the entire construction project, including the foundation, the pedestal, and the reassembly of the statue.

While the statue was still under construction and nearing completion, France had raised a substantial amount of money to ship the statue to America, but America had done little to get the statue across the Atlantic. The American press was very critical of the project and its cost. Congress had rejected a bill appropriating $100,000 for the base. The governor of New York vetoed a grant for $50,000. There was much publicity surrounding the cost and how to fund the project. Many outside of New York considered this to be a New York project and refused to participate in the fundraising.

In a letter dated December 19, 1882, Bartholdi wrote to the chairman of the Committee in America, "Our work advances. The Statue commences to reach above the houses, and by next spring we shall see it over-looking the entire city, as the large monuments of Paris now do."

Senator William M. Evarts held fundraising events, but by 1884 only $182,491 had been collected because the public was still apathetic to the cause. The worst part about this was that all but $3,000 of the money had been spent. A Hungarian immigrant by the name of Joseph Pulitzer had become a successful journalist and married a wealthy woman, who owned the financial newspaper called the *World* and another newspaper called the *St. Louis Post Dispatch*. When he saw that the project was nearly dead, Pulitzer took advantage of the opportunity to do three things: (1) raise funds for the statue; (2) increase his newspaper's circulation; (3) blast the rich for their selfishness.

Pulitzer set the fundraising at $100,000. With his newspaper, he targeted the working class to embarrass the rich. He firmly made his point that the statue was not for New York, but it would be a monument for all America. Being a journalist, he knew that people loved to have their names listed in the paper and that they would do whatever it took to do so. He cleverly advertised that he would list the names of every person in the *World* who contributed to the cause of erecting the statue, regardless of the contributed amount. He wrote, "The *World* is the people's paper and it now appeals to the people to come forward and raise the money (for the statue's pedestal). The statue was paid for by the masses of the French people. Let us respond in like manner. Let us not wait for the millionaires to give this money. It is not a gift from the millionaires of France to the millionaires of America, but a gift of the whole people of France to the whole people of America."

African American newspapers joined in the effort, encouraging their readers to contribute to a monument that would, in part, commemorate the end of slavery. Little did the African Americans know that the statue was sculptured to resemble them. The Lady's facial features surprised the media and multitudes. The dam opened and monies rushed in from all quarters of the United States. Grandmothers and children opened their piggybanks. On August 11, 1885, the front page of the *World* proclaimed, "One Hundred Thousand Dollars!" The goal had been reached and slightly exceeded. In May of 1886, twenty-three years after the slaves had been set free; the Lady of liberty began to rise in America.

Respecting, honoring, and cheering the obliteration of slavery in the United States, France sent from the people a statue representing the freedom that all people would receive after coming to the New World. The French government supplied a vessel, the *Isere*, which transported the statue to the United States. Packed with 214 specially-constructed cases, all numbered so that the Lady would be assembled correctly, the *Isere* left Rouen, France, on May 21, 1886. It arrived on June 15, 1886, at Sandy Hook, at the entrance of New York Harbor. On June 17, 1886, after the title papers were handed to General Stone, the vessel docked at Bedloe's Island (where Bartholdi had previously suggested).

Six months later, on October 25, 1886, Bartholdi and his wife, accompanied by Count Ferdinand-Marie de Lesseps, arrived in America. Edouard de Laboulaye had died a few years earlier and would never see Lady Liberty erected. At Bedloe's Island, Bartholdi, surrounded by newspaper reporters, simply said, "The dream of my life is accomplished."

On October 28, 1886, Bartholdi stood atop the head of the statue with a cord to drop the French tricolor veil from the face of the statue. The plans to unveil the Lady also included a young boy that would give him the signal to pull the cord. While Senator William Evarts was speaking, he paused to take a breath, and the little boy, thinking the senator was finished, waved the handkerchief. Bartholdi pulled the cord and unveiled the statue's gleaming copper face to a multiplicity of people in the area and to the world in general. Evarts sat down. When President Grover Cleveland took the podium, he stated, "We will not forget that Liberty has made here her home, nor shall her chosen altar be neglected."

Black Americans should not forget Bartholdi's sacrifice to risk his own reputation as a great sculptor by giving America, which was a majority white controlled country, a statue of freedom that resembled the ones to whom freedom was denied.

Engraved on the pedestal on which the statue stands is the following famous poem by the Jewish poet Emma Lazarus (1849-1887). At the time this poem was written, many immigrants were coming into America. It spoke not of asylum, but of the opportunity of becoming sons and daughters to inherit the prosperity this land had to offer. With her torch pointed to the heavens and with the gleam from her brazen face, the Lady spoke to all that were oppressed and said to them, as one that had been oppressed: join me in offering hope to the oppressed, the tired, the beaten, and the poor.

"The New Colossus"
By Emma Lazarus

Not like the brazen giant of Greek fame,
With conquering limbs astride from land to land;
Here at our sea-washed, sunset gates shall stand
A mighty woman with a torch whose flame
Is imprisoned lightning, and her name
Mother of Exiles. From her beacon-hand
Glows worldwide welcome; her mild eyes command
The air-bridged harbor that twin cities frame.
"Keep ancient lands your storied pomp!" cries she with silent
lips.
"Give me your tired your poor,
Your huddled masses yearning to breathe free,
The wretched refuse of your teeming shore.
Send these, the homeless, tempest-tossed to me,
I lift my lamp beside the golden door!"

In her left arm, Lady Liberty holds a tablet inscribed with the date of the Declaration of Independence: July 4, 1776. In her right arm is the torch of freedom. In the completed statue, the shackle, which Liberty symbolically has broken, lies in front of her right foot, the heel of which is raised as in walking. The shackle disappears beneath the draperies and reappears in front of her left foot, the end link modeled to appear broken. This cannot be seen by people that visit the Lady. In this description, the mystery is revealed regarding the person that Bartholdi had in mind while sculpting the statue. It can only be a slave that has broken the chains and is now free.

Black Americans, if they wish to brag about their place in this United States of America, can brag about the fact that a national symbol that represents freedom is a female of the black ethnic group. This statue is in the form of a black person. I am proud that America accepted this statuesque form to tell others from different parts of the world that this country is the land of the free and the home of the brave. The very people that were hated and shamed were now the pride of freedom. Lady Liberty is the mother of freedom who holds in her powerful right hand the torch for all that are oppressed and seeking refuge and a better way of living.

Out of obscurity and into prominence with the remainder of our brothers and sisters of the human race, came the African slave woman to stand and say to Blacks in America, as well as to all Americans, "Your trials may be many, your travel may have been long, but do not give up. When you come to me, I will point your head up to heaven that you may continue to pray for peace in your fight for total freedom. I will always stand free on this American soil, and so shall you. In this be strong."

Dimensions of Liberty:	Feet	Inches
Height from base to torch	151	1
Foundation of pedestal to torch	305	1
Heel to top of head	111	1
Length of hand	16	5
Index finger	8	0
Size of finger, 13 x 10"		
Head from chin to cranium	17	3
Right arm, length	42	0
Width of mouth	3	0
Height of granite pedestal	89	0
Height of foundation	65	0

Total weight of statue—250,000 pounds (225 tons)

CHAPTER 14
STARTING OVER WITH PERILS

FREEDOM AFTER THE EMANCIPATION

The Proclamation to emancipate the slaves only gave the slaves more hope that they could live in America without being the property of fellow Americans. After the Union soldiers announced to them that they were free, they could only look up to heaven and pray for protection from the ones that could not accept their freedom. Slavery had been cruel; defending the right to live free would be equally tough. The slave owners and their business partners had lost their economic base. This loss of wealth stoked the passion of slave owners and their friends to hatred for the slaves. The hatred for the new citizens was not because of the color of their skin; it was because of economics and equality.

The government promised the slaves seven acres and a mule. This promise was riddled with problems: mules could not reproduce, and the land was constantly being stolen because the black Americans could not read and did not have the manpower to protect themselves.

The turn of the nineteenth century saw black Americans still fighting for their identity and respect. In other words, they were Americans only in title. Those that had the power to make it right (the government, white churches, white preachers, and white politicians) failed miserably. If the major churches had voiced their opposition to the treatment of the new citizens, Blacks would have advanced much faster than what they were given credit for. Sadly, the churches (preaching from the Word of God) condoned the mistreatment of Blacks. In the early twentieth century, the ones that hindered the progress of black Americans were prominent members of churches. In the North, they had fought to free the slaves, but for the most part the new citizens were kept out of the best schools and jobs. In the South, white masters no longer owned them, but white southerners fought to keep them out of the best schools and jobs. Both the North and the South tried extremely hard to keep these new citizens from advancing as American citizens. As is always the case when people are insecure about themselves; they usually try to imprison others.

Except for not having a slave master, in most cases the black Americans fared no better at the turn of the twentieth century than the black African slaves of the previous centuries:

- They could not interact with Whites.
- They could not go to their events.
- They could not eat at their restaurants, even though they cooked the food.
- They could not use the same drinking facilities.
- They could not use the same bathrooms.
- They could not sit with them on pleasure outings.
- They had to hold their heads down when speaking to them.
- They could sing as well as they could sing but were not allowed to sing with them.
- They could play sports just as well but were not allowed to play with or compete against them.
- They could not go to school with them but could clean their schools.

- Most of them could not play with their children in public, but some of black women were employed to rear and care for their children. The white children even sucked the breasts of black women. I saw this with my own eyes in the twentieth century.

- They could attend their churches but had to sit in quarantined areas.

- The men never could grow up; they were always considered "boys."

- The adults had to honor Whites from birth to death with "yes sir and yes ma'am."

- They became criminals just because a white woman decided to cry wolf.

- They could not marry white women, but they slept with black women in shameful ways.

- Justice was not for them. Barabbas committed the crime, but they had to pay for it.

- Black teachers did not have the right tools to reprogram their youth from that sick and damnable system of slavery, and it was too late to do anything with the adults. Then the public laughed at them because they could not read and speak well.

They stuck black families in the back woods, they crammed them in the inner city with parents that were uneducated and destitute, and told them that if they could get to school they could learn to read. So they had to walk miles to and from school. Is it any wonder why most of them never finished school? Because of poverty, is it any wonder why they had to leave school early to help Mom and Dad survive? Is it any wonder why they spoke the dialect of slaves? This form of speech was called Ebonics. It was not a proper dialect; it was a language to get by on until they could have equal access to good education. I was offended when black Americans proposed a bill to teach black American children the language of slaves. We are not slaves; we are Americans. We were cheated; why cheat ourselves?

They took polls to show that Blacks were academically below or behind Whites. What a revelation that was! If you take a pair of white twins, give one of the twins twelve years of good education, withhold education from the other one, and then stick a California Achievement Test (CAT) in front of them, I guarantee you that even though they both are white, the educated one will score higher than the uneducated one. This was a brilliant scheme to teach black kids they were not as intelligent as Whites. According to the following example, this was similar to the scheme France tried to cook up to find out why some of its youth were on the same playing field but not running at the same speed as the others.

France hired Alfred Binet and his colleagues to identify the mental incompetence among their school children. They thought that the findings would help to improve their educational system. In 1895 Binet and his colleagues astounded the educational arena with a landmark paper in which they argued that testing the ability of one's senses or movement was not as good as testing the psychological processes thought to be involved in intelligence. Binet said intelligence operated at its own level and was independent of movement and the senses. He suggested testing memory, imagery, attentiveness, imagination, verbal comprehension, mechanical ability, suggestibility, artistic appreciation, moral sensitivity, distance-judging, and muscular endurance. These tests seemed to work, and France was able to identify mentally deficient children.[43] As with any group that has formed its conclusion before an in-depth, comprehensive investigation can be done, France was subjective in that it did not circulate an important finding of Binet's work.

The untouted finding of Alfred Binet's work was that people's learning ability could be enhanced or hindered by many factors, one of which was environment. Keep in mind that black Americans, for the most part, had been placed in an environment that prevented their progenitors from learning. After Binet died in 1911, William Stern, a German psychologist, coined the phrase *intelligence quotient* (IQ). He divided a child's mental age by chronological age and multiplied by 100 to determine the child's capability for learning. Initially the tests unexpectedly proved the opposite of what they had hoped, for girls outscored the boys. So they revised their methodology so that the "superior" gender would not look like idiots.

Many years later, a study published in 1949 by Marie Skodak and H. M. Sheels, showed that babies born to mothers with low IQs but who were adopted into upper class homes, grew up to have higher IQs than their mothers. Surprise! Binet was right after all. Environment had much to do with learning ability. In 1965 black Americans were removed from environments that restricted their learning and moved to much better learning environments. Once black Americans have cleansed their system of the poison injected into their subconscious by the government, plantation owners, and the segregated churches and schools, they will be able to match the Whites in any achievement tests. But some in government want us to judge ourselves prior to the 1960s. No thanks! We can accept our lack, but we will never accept inferiority.

Intelligence belongs to the human race: we write, invent, build, and reconstruct. Europe sanctioned Charles Darwin to go ahead with his foolish theory about how the human race entered this world. Darwin wrote—but did not truly believe—that man evolved from apes. Based on this theory, Europeans concocted the idea that they were the superior race, not understanding that there was only one race of people. If they had read the Bible, they would not have been tricked into thinking that we came from apes. This ape teaching made a monkey out of them by trying to make others believe they were inferior to Europeans. Before Europe became the world superpower, many nations and cultures held to this same belief only to discover they were grossly wrong.

Our current President George W. Bush has put in motion a "no child left behind" policy. This is a great policy. If it is followed properly, then all the public and private schools will be impartial to all students, and the black kids will finally catch up. If school boards really want to find out how Blacks are progressing, let them compare the statistics of sixty years ago with today. Blacks are equal to Whites in intelligences. This is why the Preamble states, "All men are created equal." Having access to knowledge and education and a good learning environment both at home and at school makes all the difference. If a people's learning ability is taken away, it is scientifically evident that their offspring will incur those same awful mental disabilities. It will take generations of educated offspring to heal themselves. We can see this happening before our eyes.

BLACK AMERICANS ARE BRILLIANT PEOPLE

To help those who still cannot come to terms with the fact that intelligence is not determined by different colors of skin, I believe a look at history through objective eyes will shed a little light. The white slave masters told the black African slaves that they had neither souls nor the ability to learn. After emancipation, the bosses told black American ex-slaves they would never be like the Whites. And because of the threat of death, most of them believed it. From the early 1900s until 1968, both the government and corporate America told black Americans that, although they were equal, they had to remain separate. By saying this they still placed them in an inferior category, which ultimately meant black Americans would never be equal to white Americans. But all men are created equal; therefore, we all came from the same intelligent source: Adam and Eve.

Genesis 3 tells of Adam's superior intellectual ability to name things according to their sound and shapes. Genesis 5 tells of Adam's descendents' intellectual abilities to invent different things.

Blacks are descendents of that same intellect. It is impossible for intelligent people, even if they are suppressed, not to be the inventive people God made them to be. While honor should be bestowed upon the ones who gave us many life-sustaining supports and equipment, one will receive no glory by trying to compare the success of color versus color. It is a shame for any people to try to hide the accomplishment of another people because of color or ethnicity. The Blacks in America have contributed much by their intellect. Some American textbooks leave out the history of the great and marvelous inventions of African slaves and black Americans for fear of having it said of the immigrants from Europe that they did not build this country on their own.

Why does it hurt to say that neither you nor your ancestry discovered or invented everything? Why cannot honor be given to all the laborers? The answer is hurtful and condescending: fear, ignorance, and self-centeredness. That same superior European attitude that was defeated by George Washington and stamped out by the Declaration of Independence has been resuscitated by textbook editors. Having this attitude is like people who keep their loved one's ashes on the mantle for years. Get over it. The loved one is not coming back and will not be making any more contributions to your life. I say to the textbook editors, get over it and stop holding on to dead things. Commendably, most Whites in America do not hold to the same philosophy they did prior to the year 1968.

Americans, especially black Americans, as a whole do not know the achievements of their forefathers that invented many great things in this country. The people I will briefly mention should be praised for what they did in the era in which they accomplished it. Success should always be heralded when it arises out of obscurity. In the twenty-first century it is easy for all to get their inventions on the market. All you need is about $7,000 and some perseverance. Reality television shows help those who have what it takes to get their inventions on the market. The door is wide open for us today, but it was not that way many years ago.

The list below gives credit to the black Americans who helped the world become a better place.

George Washington Carver (1865?-1943) was an American scientist, educator, humanitarian, and former slave. Carver developed hundreds of products from peanuts, sweet potatoes, pecans, and soybeans. His discoveries greatly improved the agricultural output and the health of southern farmers. Before this, the main southern crop was cotton. Carver also invented products such as a rubber substitute, adhesives, foodstuffs, dyes, pigments, and many others.

George Crum (January 25, 1918-August 2, 1858) invented the potato chip in 1853. Crum was a Native American/African American chef at the Moon Lake Lodge resort in Saratoga Springs, New York. French fries were popular at the restaurant, and one day a diner complained that the fries were too thick. Although Crum made a thinner batch, the customer was still unsatisfied. Crum finally made fries that were too thin to eat with a fork, hoping to annoy the extremely fussy customer. The customer, surprisingly enough, was happy, and potato chips were invented!

Clatonia Joaquin Dorticus was an African American inventor who received many patents. He invented an apparatus for applying dyes to the sides of the soles and heels of shoes (Patent #535,820, March 19, 1895), a machine for embossing (contouring the paper of) photographs (Patent #537,442, April 16, 1895), a device that helped develop photographs (Patent #537,968, April 23, 1895), and a leak stopper for hoses (Patent #629,315, July 18, 1899).

Philip B. Downing invented the street letter-drop mailbox with a hinged door that closed to protect the mail. Downing, an African American inventor, patented his new device on October 27, 1891 (Patent # 462,096).

Sarah E. Goode (1850-?) was a businesswoman and inventor. Goode invented the folding cabinet bed, a space saver that folded up against the wall into a cabinet. When folded up, it could be used as a desk, complete with compartments for stationery and writing supplies. Goode owned a furniture store in Chicago, Illinois, and invented the bed for people living in small apartments. Goode's patent was the first one obtained by an African American woman inventor (Patent #322,177, approved on July 14, 1885).

Lewis Howard Latimer (1848-1928) was an African American inventor who was a member of Edison's research team, which was called "Edison's Pioneers." Latimer improved the newly invented incandescent light bulb by inventing a carbon filament (which he patented in 1881).

Elijah McCoy (1843 or 1844-1929) was a mechanical engineer and inventor. McCoy's high-quality industrial inventions (especially his steam engine lubricator) were the basis for the expression "the real McCoy," meaning the real, authentic, or high-quality thing.

Booker T. Washington (April 5, 1856 – Nov. 14, 1915) was an American educator, author and leader of the African American community. He was born into slavery in southwestern Virginia. After slavery was abolished he worked his way through what is now known as Hampton University, he also attend college at Wayland Seminary. He returned to Hampton as a teacher, and in 1881 became the first leader of what is now know as Tuskegee University in Alabama. Washington was a very wise educator. He realized that the only way for Blacks to obtain total freedom, in the place and era they lived, was to get a good education. Many of his colleagues disagreed with his philosophy during that time, but they would call him a prophet if they were living today.

Garrett Augustus Morgan (March 4, 1877-August 27, 1963) was an African American inventor and businessman. He was the first person to patent a traffic signal. He also developed the gas mask (and many other inventions). Morgan used his gas mask (Patent #1,090,936, 1914) to rescue miners who were trapped underground in a noxious mine. Soon after, Morgan was asked to produce gas masks for the U. S. Army.

Norbert Rillieux (March 17, 1806-October 8, 1894) was an African American inventor and engineer who invented a device that revolutionized sugar processing. Rillieux's multiple effect vacuum sugar evaporator (patented in 1864) made the processing of sugar more efficient, faster, and much safer. The resulting sugar was also superior. His apparatus was eventually adopted by sugar processing plants all around the world.

Madame C. J. Walker (December 23, 1867-May 25, 1919) was an inventor, businesswoman, and self-made millionaire. Sarah Breedlove McWilliams C. J. Walker was an African American who developed many beauty and hair care products that were extremely popular. Madame Walker started her cosmetics business in 1905. Her first product was a scalp treatment that used petroleum and a hot comb. Sarah later invented a system for straightening hair. She added Madame to her name and began selling her new "Walker System" door-to-door. Walker soon added a hair-growing ointment and other cosmetic products to her line. The products were very successful, and she soon had many saleswomen called "Walker Agents," who sold her products door-to-door.

In 1891 Dr. Daniel Hale Williams (1856-1931) established what would become the oldest freestanding black-owned hospital in the United States: Provident Hospital and Medical Center in Chicago. Two years later Dr. Williams performed the first successful open-heart surgery.

Where would we be without these inventions? If your answer is "lost," then start now by praising the inventors. Not only did slaves and former slaves show their intelligence by inventing, they showed it through academic, theater, law, sports and many other things. Below are just a few great events that show the accomplishments of black Americans.

1896—Mary Church Terrell became the first president of the National Association of Colored Women, working for educational and social reform in an effort to end racial discrimination.

1903—W.E.B. DuBois published *The Souls of Black Folk*, in which he declared, "The problem of the Twentieth Century is the problem of the color-line," and discussed the dual identity of black Americans.

1905—The Niagara Movement, an organization of black intellectuals led by W.E.B. DuBois, was founded. The group called for full political, civil, and social rights for African Americans and was the forerunner of the National Association for the Advancement of Colored People.

1914—Sam Lucas became the first black actor to star in a full-length Hollywood film. Lucas played Tom in Uncle Tom's Cabin.

1916—Fritz Pollard was the first black football player to be named "All-American" as well as the first black player to appear in a Rose Bowl. He went on to become the first African American head coach in the NFL when he headed the Akron Pros in 1921 and was later inducted into the Pro Football Hall of Fame in 1954.

The Blood Bank—Dr. Charles Richard Drew (1904-1950) was an American medical doctor and surgeon who started the idea of a blood bank and a system for the long term preservation of blood plasma (he found that plasma kept longer than whole blood). His ideas revolutionized the medical profession and saved many, many lives. Dr. Drew set up and operated the blood plasma bank at the Presbyterian Hospital in New York City, New York. Dr. Drew's project was the model for the Red Cross's system of blood banks, of which he became the first director.

Black American citizens owe themselves to prosper in this prosperous land. The Africans who were enslaved on *La Armistad* were set free after a lengthy ordeal from 1839-1842, but they had no desire to stay in America. While waiting to see if they would be tried for murder or exonerated, they were treated with care and even taught English by Yale students. When the news came that they were free and could return to Africa, they did not hesitate to say goodbye to America. Only one out of that group ever returned to the United States; her name was Sarah.[44] For Africans such as these, America was not their home. But for the ones who labored and suffered here, America was their home. Many of the former slaves who had the finances to do so thought it not right to spit on the blood of those who died to make it possible for them to enjoy this land. It would have been very easy for them to return to their native land, but they had a mission greater than personal achievement and freedom. They, as the progenitors, had a mission to instill faith and confidence in the bloodlines of the ones who would be born in the future. They wanted me to know many years later, that the flag of this United States of America was ours by default. (Thank you, forefathers.)

The Shakeup in the Churches Baptized in the Holy Spirit

Regardless of the rough and degrading start black Americans had to go through, the spirit of the American flag was still alive. Only this time it was alive in black Americans. Emancipation gave them power. The thought in their heart was, "If I'm equal, then why am I treated as through I'm inferior?" With the assistance of the freedom Proclamation, they now could fight for themselves. The warfare of the black Americans was not about whom they could shoot and kill; rather, it was about education and being integrated into the economy as wage earners. After coming out of slavery and being denied a good education, they needed a different type of help. They needed something living on the inside of them from God.

It is evident that America has the spirit of the two sons of Joseph (the Prince of Egypt), Ephraim and Manasseh. Therefore, all Americans have the rights to be prosperous and strong. They must also be servants of God, because their father was a man of faith. The church started this government and country; therefore, the church had to be the one that removed the hindrance from some of its citizens. Success was not achieved overnight or in a few years. The blueprint for success had to be drawn up to anticipate a lengthy process. Every American must have an opportunity to enjoy the prosperity that the flag promised. The oppressed citizens would be vindicated because the flag represented the God of liberty and blessings. How could those that were limited, but believed in the same God, get help from God when it seemed as if God was on the side of the oppressors? Did not all of them go to church? What could cause an awakening in the church to help all the children of Ephraim and Manasseh to prosper?

It would be the baptism of the Holy Ghost. "But [all of] you shall receive power when the Holy Spirit has come upon you; and you shall be witnesses to Me both in Jerusalem, and in all Judea and Samaria, and to the end of the earth" (Acts 1:8). This was Jesus' command to His disciples. The power they received from Him changed their lives forever; it gave them power to help change the live of others. This power gave them superior intellect. They opened their mouth, and knowledge they had not learned came out. This power caused them to start a spiritual family that would include all mankind: male, female, Blacks, Whites, Yellows, and Browns. They loved God before they received the baptism of the Holy Spirit, but there was this "separate but equal" mentality. The ends of the earth were the lands beyond Palestine, and they had to go beyond their ethnic group to a people that did not look, act, or talk like them. They went throughout the known world preaching the resurrection of Christ, healing the sick, casting out devils, and bringing all nationalities into the one true ecclesia of God in Christ.

After the second century, this supernatural power was lost in the churches to those that were in the Dark Ages, the Renaissance, and the middle 1800s. It was not until the late 1890s that people began to seek the Lord for His power. (Even though God brought dramatic change in the 1500s, one part of His divine favor was yet to come.) The major Christian religions in the world were Catholic, Baptist, Methodist, Lutheran, Presbyterian, Calvinist, Puritan, and the Quakers. Regardless of the prefix or suffix attached to other church buildings, these were the major religions at that time. Each one of these denominations had its own color line. Whites could not mingle with Blacks, and God help the poor black person who strayed too close to the Whites. The philosophy taught at the time was that God was for all, but not if all worshiped together. Even though He made man (male and female) in His own image, men had drawn a line between themselves then dared others to cross it. After the Emancipation Proclamation of 1863, black Americans began to organize and distance themselves from white churches. But, they kept the mainstream theology of the white churches.

Black leaders such as Daniel Payne and Theophilus Gould Steward established missions in the South to help Blacks establish their own churches. Churches such as the African Methodist Episcopal (AME) and African Methodist Episcopal Zion (AMEZ) were established during this time. In 1894 black Baptists formed the National Baptist Convention. Also during this period, many denominations became involved in the Holiness Movement. They believed in a very strict moral life and dress code. These holiness people began to pray for the sick and believed God for miracles. But, there was still this color line.

In the early 1900s God prepared two men that never knew each other to change the way church members worshiped and interacted. One was a one-eyed, moderately educated black man named William J. Seymour, whom the *Los Angles Times* (1906) called illiterate. The other was a white man named Frank Bartleman. He was an educated newspaper writer. He had no money, a wife, and some children, and one of the children was very sick. After many hardships that were laid on both men, their travels in life took them to the same place at almost the same time. Both of these men were seeking the Lord beyond the theology of their denominations.

Then it happened in America, starting in Los Angles, California, in April of 1906, at a small mission on Azusa Street. Blacks and Whites were worshiping together in one accord, and suddenly they were all filled with the Holy Spirit and began to speak with other tongues (another language) as the Spirit gave them utterance. This was called the Pentecostal experience. These were people who had come out from the dead churches of all denominations. The noise that came from this mission was heard abroad, and many people, just by hearing it, were filled with the Holy Spirit and power. This was the same spiritual outpouring that had occurred over two thousand years ago in Jerusalem.

William Seymor

Frank Bartleman

Azusa Street 1906

The two leaders of the early Pentecostal movement in America

Just as the men and women of Jerusalem were mocked and laugh at, so were the worshipers at Azusa Street. The phenomena of the Spirit-filled speaking in another language, healing the sick, loving, and spreading the truth about Jesus, spread from this West Coast town of America to the East Coast and then to Europe. Most of the world was affected.

Charles Parham, a major leader of the Apostolic Holiness movement, did not believe in integrated worshiping. He was greatly taken back when he saw the supernatural power with which

William Seymour ignored his request to segregate himself from this church practice. Prior to Seymour's Spirit baptism, he had obeyed Parham, but this time he had power from God that caused him to resist all temptation to segregate from white Christians. The baptism of the Holy Spirit had imparted supernatural knowledge and boldness to Seymour. After this outpouring of the Spirit of God, American church fellowship and worship would never be the same.

From this time forward, Blacks and Whites that believed in this experience fellowshiped together on a continuous basis. Other denominations continued their separate but equal status. You may want to take notice of the churches that believe in the baptism of the Holy Spirit and the ones that do not. In the churches that believe in this experience, you will notice that there is a heavy mixture of Whites, Blacks, and others worshiping together. I believe this happens because the Spirit of God delivers believers from the mentality of skin color and gives them the spiritual insight to fellowship with all of God's children. Where the Spirit of God is there is liberty. I am only speaking about America as a whole. These churches that consider themselves separate but equal are dead as empty church pews.

The Pentecostal experience helped changed the attitude of many black and white preachers. This Pentecostal fire gave power to as many as would submit themselves to God so He could cause the spirit of Ephraim and Manasseh (prosperity) to arise in the United States for all people. God was preparing this country for wealth like they had never seen before. But in order for Him to bring it to pass, He had to give hope to all of Ephraim's and Manasseh's offspring. So the latter rain (Holy Spirit outpouring in the early 1900s) came to that which was void. God caused the light to shine in a dark place, and life came like America had never known before.

The Azusa Street ministry started something great. It had to come to pass so true change of equality could be given to all that were under the banner of the flag. The Azusa Street ministry lasted until 1909 when God had to stop the glory of Azusa Street so that the creature would not be worshiped more than the Creator. One must understand that God will not give His glory to another. The mission had to cease because God needed to start churches with this experience all over America. Worship is a universal obeisance; therefore, Blacks and Whites had to worship together in America if true change was to come. True change was exactly what happened.

New denominations began to form, and church membership grew. Black preachers started to enjoy the power of church ownership and the true freedom of worship. Little by little God was breaking the yokes of the white preachers' power that had kept black preachers in fear. From 1909 to the early 1930s, black pastors set up their own church organizations, and there was nothing the white ministers could do about it. If all men were created equal, God Himself had to make that statement clear. When God makes a statement, no one can change it. God made the statement, and many white males and females submitted themselves to black clergy leadership. For the first time in America's history, black American males were leaders over Whites. The irony of this was that it was in the church where Christ had echoed years before that in Him all would be the same. In the 1920s some of these white ministers left the churches that had black leaders, but they did not return to the dead churches of the past. They established other spirit-filled church organizations, and many black Americans found freedom in majority white churches.

Quotes from Former Slaves and Their Descendents

Motivational speakers use quotes to get their point across in the hope that someone will grasp their meaning and become a better person or do a better job in the discipline they have chosen or that has been chosen for them. The following quotes from great former slaves give me a greater appreciation for my fight to let the Blacks in America know that we do not have to hate to get ahead; we have to pray and walk past those that do hate. We need to keep in remembrance the final words of the Emancipation Proclamation: "And upon this act, sincerely believed to be an act of justice, warranted by the Constitution, upon military necessity, I invoke the considerate judgment of mankind, and the gracious favor of Almighty God."

Benjamin Banneker: "One universal Father hath given to us all . . . Endowed us with the same faculties . . . We are all of the same family."

-From a letter dated August 19, 1791, to Thomas Jefferson

Aaron Douglas: "I refuse to compromise and see blacks as anything less than a proud and majestic people."

Frederick Douglass: "Every tone [of the songs of the slaves] was a testimony against slavery, and a prayer to God for deliverance from chains."

Langston Hughes: "I swear to the Lord, I still can't see why Democracy means everybody but me."

Barbara Jordan: " 'We, the people.' It is a very eloquent beginning. But when that document was completed . . . I was not included in that 'We, the people.' I felt somehow for many years that George Washington and Alexander Hamilton just left me out by mistake. But through the process of amendment, interpretation and court decision, I have finally been included in 'We, the people.' "

Harriet Tubman: "I had reasoned this out in my mind; there was one or two things I had a right to, liberty or death; if I could not have one, I would have the other . . . I should fight for my liberty as long as my strength lasted, and when the time comes for me to go, the Lord would let them take me."

Booker T. Washington: "No race can prosper till it learns that there is as much dignity in tilling a field as in writing a poem."

LAST STEP TO COMPLETE FREEDOM—CIVIL RIGHTS

The early 1930s to the 1950s were not easy times for Blacks economically. White women were making some progress, but they were still treated as indentured servants or slaves. Blacks enjoyed public religious freedom, but their civil rights were suppressed. Both religious and civil rights are needed for complete freedom for the whole person.

America was growing spiritually, but it was dying politically. The federal government had pushed the Emancipation Proclamation and The Constitution under the expensive floor rugs in the White House. Black Americans were deceitfully denied their basic rights to function in this free society. They had waited for two hundred years for life, liberty, and the pursuit of happiness, but it was withheld from them. The church advised its members to keep praying and waiting on God. Their patience was seeping out, and they were growing weary of the injustices that were allowed by those that were elected to protect them. For example, J.W. Milam and Roy Bryant killed Emmett Till, a fourteen-year-old black Chicagoan, for whistling at a white woman. They were acquitted by an all-white jury. In *Look* magazine the two perpetrators bragged about the incident. The government allowed these men to fuel the hope of others who may have wished to do the same to other Blacks.

Hiding behind small cells and walls, black militants and hippy groups were forming in retaliation to the injustices. America was getting ready to experience another war that could only spell national disaster. Young black educated men and women saw no light of justice at the end of the tunnel and decided it was time to make a statement: "Give me liberty or give me death." Unlike the Civil War of the 1860s, the 1960s included new weapons and new technology. If the militant groups stockpiled weapons arsenals across the country, they could inflict damages such as America has never seen. On the other hand, in retaliation to the forwardness of the militant groups, the government had new destructive weapons. And if it decided to use them on its own citizens, America's progress would suffer a setback for many years. Many leaders in the federal government did not understand this serious situation and would have sanctioned another civil war.

If this was God's country for purposes of evangelizing the world and a light of hope for all that accepted His grace and city of refuge for all mankind, God had to raise up another Abraham Lincoln that would be peaceful but fearless. This person must understand several things: they could be killed; they could not fight against their own country (a house divided against itself cannot stand); their followers must have the same peaceful goals; they must not expect glory; and they must glorify the Lord God. Many leaders had risen up to proclaim themselves the black man's savior, but America was sick, and God needed a person that would bring healing. He would not use a militant to carry out His plan for peace. To reiterate, this country had started from the church, it proclaimed its independence by the church, and now its final healing must come from the church.

Dr. Martin Luther King Jr.[45]

From 1955-1968 God used a man with the spirit of Martin Luther and the spirit of Abraham Lincoln. His name was Martin Luther King, Jr. of Atlanta, Georgia. After he had been properly educated and encouraged by fellow black leaders and clergy, he was convinced that it was time for Ephraim's and Manasseh's children to possess that which had been left out. Even though he was a Baptist preacher, King preached civil rights, and his congregation was the American public and the government. The peace marches, the sit-ins, and the refusal to sit at the back of the bus were things done in name of peace to let America know that the flag was not there just to give prosperity to Whites; it was there for all Americans.

America's Civil Rights Movement was in full motion. Many people died during this time for the cause of the flag. Some had to die so that the future could offer *all* American citizens health and wealth. But many more lives would have been lost if it was not for divine providence. God led Martin Luther King Jr. in the spirit of wisdom to avoid a national catastrophe. In 1964 with the passing of the Civil Rights laws, and the Voting Rights Act of 1965, all Americans could now look forward to enjoying what some Americans had been so privileged to have for years. When the government truly honored the meaning of the flag, it opened the door of wealth for all of it citizens.

Martin Luther King Jr. prevailed as a leader of opportunity to get the United States government to recognize that it was withholding from a significant portion of its citizens the freedom to enjoy the wealth that God had granted it. Not seeing progress come as fast as he and others would like, and knowing that death was imminent because of the many death threats on his life, King came to the realization that he would never see harmony exist in America in his lifetime. But he proclaimed in one of the greatest speeches ever recorded, that he had a dream that "unity" would come.

He stated, I have a dream that one day on the red hills of Georgia the sons of former slaves and the sons of former slave owners will be able to sit down together at the table of brotherhood. I have a dream that one day even the state of Mississippi, a state sweltering with the heat of injustice, sweltering with the heat of oppression, will be transformed into an oasis of freedom and justice. I have a dream that my four little children will one day live in a nation where they will not be judged by the color of their skin but by the content of their character.

I have a dream today.

I have a dream that one day down in Alabama, with its vicious racists, with its governor having his lips dripping with the words of interposition and nullification - one day right there in Alabama little black boys and black girls will be able to join hands with little white boys and white girls as sisters and brothers.

I have a dream today.

I have a dream that one day every valley shall be exalted and every hill and mountain shall be made low, the rough places will be made plain, and the crooked places will be made straight, and the glory of the Lord shall be revealed and all flesh shall see it together.

Dr. King spoke not of a vision that comes to one who is weary from a tiresome journey or the flash of a subconscious hope while one is in a deep sleep, but he spoke of a reality that was first proclaimed in 1776 and that the Declaration of Independence, the Constitution, and the United States flag had already granted, but that was disallowed by those that would gain from suppressing that reality in others. America can no longer afford to dream while we celebrate Dr. King's dream. We must respect each other in order to enjoy the wealth that this great country affords us together.

Dr. King's dream was based on the principle of freedom for all Americans. It gave others the impetus to work out how to put the pieces of the puzzle together. There comes a time when dreams that are true visions must come true. America must stop celebrating the profound "I Have A Dream" speech without any anticipation that it will come true. While many Whites are trying to move forward, many Blacks are afraid that the "I Have a Dream" speech will come true with all its intangibles. We are fixed on the celebration and not the end reality. It must come true, and it has. Dr. King's dream primarily dealt with removing fallacious philosophies held by some government officials.

On December 5, 2002, Trent Lott remarked, "I want to say this about my state: When Strom Thurmond ran for president, we voted for him. We're proud of it. And if the rest of the country had followed our lead, we wouldn't have had all these problems over all these years, either." Lott is no longer the majority leader because he failed to realize that the philosophies of segregation and racism are dead in the federal government. One needs only to look at the political, economical, administrative, social, financial, corporate, and relational changes in the landscape of our country. An objective look at these changes for many will provide a solid conviction that King's dream has come true, and all the components are in motion.

As I look backward into the past and forward into the future, I have a dream that someday from border to border, from coast to coast, from state to state, and from city to city, we Americans will connect by holding hands simultaneously across this country in an unbroken chain, to testify of our created purpose of unity and strength. Blacks, Whites, Reds, and Yellows, religious and nonreligious, males and females, boys and girl, rich and poor, the well and the sick singing with one accord, "This Land and is my land, this Land is your land . . . "

CHAPTER 15

MOVING FORWARD—BECOMING
A BETTER AMERICAN

ONE NATION—MANY PEOPLE

In the beginning God created one male and one female. The makeup of the female came directly from the male. She was bone of his bone and flesh of his flesh. She had the same DNA, making them truly one. Scientists agree that every human being has a similar DNA trait that links us to one person that lived on this earth. Bio-anthropologists call it Eve. The first male and female were given the ability to procreate after their own kind. Each person from that union has the same capability to reproduce others like themselves. After these progenitors had migrated into extremely hot, moderately hot, warm, moderately cold, or extremely cold climates, their pigmentation, height, weight, and other features adapted to those climates. After these people had adapted to one of the above environments, they lived in that environment and developed.

Each culture produces an ethnic group that lives inside the conditions to which it has adapted. Skin color, hair texture, weight, and height will be a product of this climate's living conditions.

Each ethnic group has a special talent that is unique to that group but that can be duplicated by other groups because they are all of the same genetic makeup. In hot climates the people are generally dark-skinned and with thin frames. In colder climates the people are generally fair-skinned and with heavy frames. Each group knows how to survive in its own environment. When the talents and abilities of each group are merged, greater progress is made than would be if the talents and abilities were kept inside the individual groups.

Henry Lee was a master of forensic science. Benjamin Franklin discovered the use of electricity. George Washington Carver discovered many uses for peanuts. Babe Ruth gave us a challenge to top his great performance in baseball. Jackie Robinson proved that athletic abilities belonged to the human race and not just to the fair-skinned ethnic groups. Larry Bird proved that black basketball players were not the only ones that could dazzle the basketball world. Tiger Woods proved that golf was not just a white man's game. Michael Jordan proved that a black basketball player could reinvent the game and become greater than the game itself. Bill Walton proved that white men could jump. Elvis Presley proved that a white man could dance and excite the crowd. Michael Jackson proved that a black man owned the excitement of the dance, and then he reinvented it. Bruce Lee proved that an oriental man could outwit both Whites and Blacks in martial arts.

America is blessed because we are a true melting pot. From the discovery of this land by Columbus to the arrival of the first African, the growth of this country depended on all ethnic groups. We have all nationalities living in this country, which ultimately means we have more talents living under one roof than any other country in the world. Progress seems unlimited with so many brains working to further the cause of human greatness. God's plan for progress is for His creation that gravitated into ethnic groups to come back together to work for the common good. If one group acts independently (interacting only with people that talk like them, act like them, look like them, and think like them), the nation as a whole will not prosper as fast.

Progress is made when many ideas coming from many different directions are pooled together. The corporate world calls this diversity. America has shown that through births, adoptions, and even mutations all human beings can become one nation. Acts 17:24-26 states, "God, who made the world and everything in it, since He is Lord of heaven and earth, does not dwell in temples made with hands. Nor is He worshiped with men's hands as though he needed anything, since He gives to all life, breath, and all things. And He has made from one blood every nation of men to dwell on all the face of the earth, and has determined their pre-appointed times and the boundaries of their dwellings."

A true melting pot is what we are. We now can see the immutable truth of the statement in Genesis 11:6, "And the LORD said, 'Indeed the people are one and they have all one language, and this is what they begin to do; now nothing that they propose to do will be withheld from them.' " We set out to be a people that were free to worship the God of heaven and earth. We set out to be strong. We are not falling short of progress. We are many but one spirit arising from Noah (Shem, Ham, and Japheth), Abraham (from the line of Shem), Isaac, and Jacob (Israel); Joseph married an Egyptian (from the line of Ham). So, America is Shem, Ham, and Japheth dwelling together as one people. We are one union of all nations on the earth. I believe that our melting pot identity is what inspired the following song:

"AMERICA, THE BEAUTIFUL"
By Katharine L Bates

O beautiful for spacious skies,
For amber waves of grain,
For purple mountain majesties
Above the fruited plain!

~~~

America! America!
God shed His grace on Thee,
And crown thy good with brotherhood
From sea to shining sea!

~~~

O beautiful for patriot dream
That sees beyond the years
Thine alabaster cities gleam
Undimmed by human tears!

~~~

America! America!
God shed His grace on Thee,
And crown thy good with brotherhood
From sea to shining sea!

CHAPTER 16
It Starts As a Child

Children are special. As adults, we remember when we were children. On our way to adulthood, we must go through proper attitude development stages to acquire love of country so we can become faithful and loyal citizens. Parents must understand that they are the ones who instill traits in their children, who will develop into good or bad citizens. Many children were raised to hate, but, thank God, some of these had mentors who were able to turn them around to love instead of hate. Many children were taught to love, but someone invaded their life, brainwashed them, and now they hate others. Proverbs 22:6 states, "Train up a child in the way he should go, and when he is old he will not depart from it." During the tender ages of childhood, parents or caregivers can mold and shape children into whatever they wish. Love and faithfulness should be put into a child. The parents are the potters, and the children are the clay. The parents put them on the potter's wheel of life, pour water on them to make them pliable, and mold them into people who are good, bad, ugly, lazy, dedicated, faithful, resentful, proud, and so forth. Most of the time, the result is from what parents put into their children.

Over time, many psychologists such as Sigmund Freud, Erik Erikson, John Bowlby, and Jean Piaget have studied children and formulated theories and assumptions about how children develop in all societies. These men developed theories about the cognitive capabilities, emotions, and actions of children during the developmental stages of their lives. The aspects we want to focus on are perception and cognition. *Perception* is the natural activity of combining sensations into meaningful patterns. *Cognition* is all processes by which humans acquire knowledge; the methods for thinking or gaining knowledge about the world. It is crucial for parents and caregivers to understand what effect they have on children's lives during early developmental stages, especially their cognitive development. Children's perception of dedication can be perfected or distorted during the early cognitive developmental stages. When they reach adulthood, they already have learned to love or hate God, people, or their country.

Parents and caregivers must choose carefully whom they allow to mentally feed the children under their care. Some people speak against the authority of parents, churches, government, and good, wholesome living. These people should not be part of the development of children. Mankind is obligated to act morally. If anyone teaches children to the contrary, one can only imagine the consequences that come from a life filled with confusion and insecurity. History has taught us what the future gives to people who forsake morality and dedication. It is vitally important for us to instill in our children dedication for godly and righteous living.

We can make anything right based on our subjective views; therefore, it is wise that we teach godly living over right living. We must not use the word *right* too loosely. Some people's perception of what is right is based on their lifestyle and not on truth. One may choose to follow this lifestyle or not. One can use the word *right* in a philosophical way to mean anything they wish. For instance, parents may feel it is okay for their child to use vile and vulgar language. However, vile and vulgar language is disrespectful and distasteful, and is an indication that the child has an angry spirit and an emotional problem.

Godliness, on the other hand, is absolutely *right*. It is an objective moral law that all people must follow. By following godliness, a person becomes dedicated to following that which is truly *right*. But when a person falls from godliness, they will practice that which is divisive and destructive, and then call it *right*. *Right* is therefore predicated on godliness.

A child comes into this world not knowing anything but having capabilities that must be nurtured by the parents or caregivers. How to act with moral character is learned through a training process that happens over time. According to Nora Newcombe, different cultures have different conceptions of the ideal child, and these beliefs determine how parents rear their children. A survey was done on how American and Japanese mothers reared their infants. The finding was that Japanese babies were less active, less vocal, and less spontaneous than American babies. However, it should be remembered that each child is reared within a particular cultural context, and that most children in each generation grow up to function well within their culture. In all cultures the primary training of parents is to bring up children to respect authority. Do not blame anyone else for the errors of your adolescents if you failed to teach them wholesome character traits. The blame is staring at you in the mirror.

RESPECTING AUTHORITY

Exodus 20:12 gave this command: "Honor your father and your mother, that your days may be long upon the land which the LORD your God is giving you." Aristotle stated we should act in accordance with virtue. Southern mothers of old would say, "Child, shut up before I kill you with something." This kept order. Everyone should believe in order. Without order the world would be chaotic, or at most nonexistent. God ordained order, and it is good. Without order we would live like a tale that keeps changing while being told. We would be like a snake that swallows its own tail until it has completely consumed itself. Individually, we cannot govern ourselves. Self-government beats women, aborts children, hangs minorities, euthanizes the sick elderly, steals from financial institutions, and changes the rules according to the situation of the day. We need government to establish order. Government is good; it is not a system dreamed up by a group of old men and women to make the youthful lives miserable. We need a good democratic government to keep order.

Children who are not taught to respect authority will eventually rebel against it. Thomas Jefferson stated, "If the children are untaught, their ignorance and vices will, in future life, cost us much dearer in their consequences than it would have done in their correction by a good education. Adore God; reverence and cherish your parents; love your neighbor as yourself; and your country more than life. Be just; be true; murmur not at the ways of Providence—and the life into which you will have entered will be one of eternal and ineffable bliss." While it is proper and lawful to eradicate child abuse and give children a future without all the psychological stresses they may incur from abuse, it is equally unlawful to take away the rights of parents and caregivers to rule over their children. Parents must *have* authority in order to train their children *about* authority. Parents are "the government" to their children. If the federal, state, or local governments wish to have law-abiding citizens, they must leave to the parents the responsibility of shaping and molding those that inevitably will be adults in the future. When I was a child, my mother and father taught me to respect my elders. They taught me to respect law enforcement. We lived in a community where everyone was your parent if they were older than you. My older sisters and brothers were due the same respect, because they became caregivers when the parents stepped out of the house. Mother would say, "So-and-so is in charge while I'm away, so you do what they tell you to do." I can remember getting spankings from my aunts and uncles for crimes I had committed against the authority of the community. We never talked back because the elders were due this great respect. If we talked back, we would get another spanking when Mom or Dad got home. (However, adults did not go around the community having a whipping party to see who could whip the most children.)

Even public school teachers were due the utmost respect. From what I remember, elementary school teachers were not afraid of the students because they had the backing of the parents. Even though we children acted "human" (which means we sometimes did bad things), we never rose up against our teachers. That is, not to the high degree we have today. I can remember with acute clarity the rod of correction that was laid on many of us kids at school. This type of corporal punishment, while painful, was a deterrent to disrupting the order of the learning environment. And if you got a whipping, you hoped and prayed that Mom or Dad did not find out about it because it would mean trouble at the home front. Respecting authority was a principle all students followed.

Elementary School Days

In August of 1964, I started my first year of education at the Almont Elementary School in Almont, Alabama. The school building was fairly new. The classes went up to the fifth grade. It was an all-black school, with all-black teachers, except for the last two years prior to the integration of 1969. One of my teachers was Mrs. Onnie Fluker. I asked if she could help me remember the teachers that taught during the time I attended. I want to mention these few people because they added so much value to me in my early years of life. To these teachers we were students, not "subjects." I appreciate the fact that they trained me well. They never let me get away with anything, even though I tried very hard. Below are the names of all that Mrs. Fluker and I could remember. We may have missed some:

Mr. Booker T. Knoxs

Mrs. Onnie Fluker
Mrs. Johnnie May Du Bose
Mrs. Fannie Massey
Mrs. Ida Massey
Mrs. Sarah Toney
Mrrs. Janie Crawford
Mrs. Mary Smitherman
Mrs. Junnie Craig-Williams
Mrs. Henderson
Mrs. Fannie Bailey
Mrs. Pauline Mixon
Mrs. Lillie Jackson
Mr. Lester Bailey
Mr. Henry Smith
Mrs. Ernestine Moss
Mr. Carl Anderson

I remembered my first grade teacher leading us in prayer and in reciting the Pledge of Allegiance each day before class began. Sometimes we sang our school theme song, "Dear School, We Love Thee and Cherish Thy Name." This was a great song, and it gave me a warm, dedicated feeling toward my school. I loved that school. I remember gathering in our small auditorium to have our special activities. It was not any different from any other school or activities. But when we sang our school theme song, we were not just moving our lips; everybody put their heart into it. It was loud and beautiful. As the teacher played and led the song, we sang as through we were one voice. I spoke to Mrs. Fluker regarding the exact wording of the song. I thank God she had an original copy in her files. The song went like this:

Dear school we love thee and cherish thy name. And to thy memories this little song we gaily sing. Kind teachers, we love you and school mates so true. Ever we'll sing of the white and the blue. Happy the hours, we live here each day. Some are for work while some that are for play. Laughter and song and some hard work to do. Ever we will sing of the white and the blue. We will try to remember the lesson that we learned, dear teacher, each day. And often we will live them as we go along life's way. (Repeat first four lines) Al-al-al-mont, Al-al-al-mont, Al-al-al-mont, Al-al-al-mont. (Author unknown)

They drilled this song in me during the tender years of my life. I can remember most of the words because I was receptive to change and growth. Many other things they taught me during my elementary days are still with me today. I remember saying the Pledge of Allegiance. With my right hand over my heart, staring at the flag near the teacher's desk, I now perceive that this was a holy moment for all of us while we stood tall and still, focused on the red, white, and blue flag, with it stars that reminded us of the heavens. In unison we would say these words,

I pledge allegiance to the Flag of the United States of America and to the republic for which it stands; one nation under God, indivisible, with liberty and justice for all. Amen.

During those moments I had this awesome feeling of freedom and commitment. As far as I was concerned, there was only one country and one school: America and Almont Elementary School.

The teachers taught us to love our parents and each other and to be respectful to all people. They taught us to obey and always give thanks. We were kids to the hilt; however, you would never hear us talking badly about the teachers, our parents, or other authority figures. When my school day was finished, I went home only to hear the same teachings. What a great reinforcement we had! Both the parents and the schools worked together to bring up children in the way they should go. If the term "it takes a village" means schools, municipalities, states, and federal authorities working behind the parents, then we had a wonderful village.

I can remember going home after school was out for the day, cutting firewood, helping my grandmother, my great grandmother, and great grandfather around the house. They taught us how to work and the importance of working. In the small community of Wilton, Alabama, all the children that could work did work. We helped each other with our work. In my small neighborhood there were about thirty boys who helped each other with everything. We were very close. There was not anything we would not do for each other. We learned how to be dedicated. The work ethic we learned as children had no less an effect on us when we became adults.

Invest good things in children while they are young. The return may be many years coming, but it will be great. You will be able to see the increasing value of your investment compared to those who refused to instill godly principles in their children.

CHAPTER 17
IT STICKS WITH YOU

In the headline news the story read that a man killed a woman and children. Another story read that a man robbed a bank and killed three. Still another read that a 25-year-old man was busted in a citywide drug raid. The interesting thing is if there is a trial, the defense attorney will say, "Your Honor, my client is innocent. His or her action was a result of many years of abuse at the hand of the mother, father, uncle, or friends. He or she was molested continuously as a child. The family had no money while growing up, and this caused my client to steal to survive as a child. My client's mental anguish and hardship created these problems he or she is now having as an adult. If my client had received psychological help as a child, we would not be having this trial or hearing today." What the attorney is saying is that what the client was trained to do in his or her childhood stuck until the client's adulthood.

A few years ago I had the privilege of acting as a religious adviser for two individuals. One was facing thirteen years in prison, the other thirty-five years. For the first case I argued that from a child this person had been seeking affection from the male figure that was never in his life. When the mother remarried, he had to fight again for attention. This, I concluded, was the reason this person did what he did. After successfully arguing that the person's crime was in part due to the neglect of his father, the judge somewhat agreed and reduced the sentence to three years.

In the second case, I sent a letter to the judge. I argued that this person did what she did because the responsibility of taking care of the family was placed on her as a child. This person obeyed her parents to the fullest. Society teaches us to obey all authorities. In her adulthood, because her parents instilled in her from a child that she was responsible for the family, she acted accordingly and committed a crime to take care of her family. Amazingly, the judge in the case was so moved by the letter that she decided to attend a class on childhood abuse. The judge conferred with the psychologist, and the term *magical thinking* was offered as an excuse as to why such a wonderful person, who was not a criminal, could commit a crime such as this. The judge sentenced this person to one day in jail. The reason given for not incarcerating this person was "it was not her fault." The ones that should have been locked up were the parents. The child that is now an adult was acting out what was instilled in her as a child.

Quality children make quality adults. While all bad things that a person does cannot be blamed on parents, caregivers, and communities, many bad habits can be traced back to how a person was taught as a child.

If we want to stop men from being abusive, then as children they must never see women being abused. If we want women not to stay in abusive situations, they must not be exposed to that type of situation as children. I grew up in a neighborhood where the men would beat the women. Mothers would say to the beaten women, "Hang in there; it will be all right after a while." Of course, it never turned out to be all right. After the poor, stupid husbands would sober up, they would promise never to do it again, but of course they lied. This would become a way of life. As we grew older, I saw in some males that same abusive mentality. They thought that this culture was a way of life. So the next generation took on this same attitude.

A way of life for a child generally stays that same way of life as they become adults. Therefore, teach a boy not to beat a girl, and teach a girl not to beat a boy. Teach a girl not to allow a boy to beat her. Teach girls that it is not right to stay in a relationship when a man beats them, whether they have children or not. They should get out of that relationship and go back home. In the olden days society taught women that the only choice they had was to remain in that situation. Families refused to take them back in their house while quoting old family traditions. However, no mother, father, brother, or sister should want to see one of his or her loved ones physically abused. This is not a "leave it alone" domestic problem that the husbands and wives have to work out while abuse is going on. This is a serious crime against love ones, and they need to know that they have help and support. A girl who knows she has a safe haven with her father and mother will be less likely to take abuse when she is an adult. It sticks with you. "Train up a child in the way he should go, and when he is old he will not depart from it." It sticks with you until you change it.

Teach children how to be dedicated, and they probably will be. I have a friend that would not give her child what we call junk food. To this day that child, who is now a young adult, will not eat junk food. This young adult is dedicated to the things he learned as a child. If we can teach a child against bad things, then we can teach them about how to do good things.

THE IMPORTANCE OF TEACHING DEDICATION

We learn how to work as a child. Working is right. Whether we receive little money, no money, or lots of money, working is good. The jobs that the men had when I was growing up were not the most glamorous jobs around, but the men worked. Their hands were cut and bruised from handling rough bark and sharp limbs from the trees they cut and carried on their backs and shoulders. Their skin was darkened and hardened from the hot sun that beat down on them six, sometimes seven days a week. Many of them worked in factories that produced lime and gravel. They itched and blistered from the sulfur in the lime, which made their black skin look gray. Regardless of how the hard labor deformed their bodies, they had families to take care of. They were dedicated to their jobs because they were dedicated to their families. They risked their lives working at these low-paying, hazardous jobs, but God was with them.

Before I became a teenager I never saw the women in my community work outside the home on jobs for which they were paid an hourly wage, jobs where money would be taken out of their pay for Social Security. However, the women did work outside the home in field jobs, picking cotton, peaches, tomatoes, peas, apples, strawberries, and other fruits and vegetables. The only other jobs the women had were in other people's houses where they cleaned, cooked, and washed clothes. Many times they worked for clothes or food, trying to make ends meet. The average family size included at least seven children. There was not much money, but the women were dedicated to their families and their homes. Children were not given away to other people because of the lack of finances, food, or clothing; mothers just did the best they could with what they had. Because of commitment and dedication, they turned what would have been a lifestyle of poverty into a lifestyle of joy and comfort. The good thing about all of this was that whether it was cutting wood, picking cotton, washing other people's clothes, or cleaning houses, I saw men and women working, and that was positive. That created a dedication for working.

CARING

We never looked for handouts. In our community the mothers and fathers of each family helped take care of one another's families. We ate at each other's houses. We wore each other's clothes. We would watch each other's siblings. We were dedicated to each other. At Christmas time and other holidays it was more than a delight to help put toys and other things together. Caring was a way of life; there was no greater human gift that could be given to a child than caring (charity). Most care organizations seek for people with these types of qualities, gifts, and dedication. An effective caregiver brings joy and happiness into the lives of the downtrodden. Caring is a quality that does not seek its own pleasure in life. It epitomizes the quote from former President John Kennedy, "Ask not what your country can do for you, but what you can do for your country."

Caring is a very tough job. Its subjects are heavy, like dead weight. The time and energy involved in managing its very nature must be accurately calculated, considered, and measured, or you will be like a person swimming in the ocean alongside a great white shark; there is no hope of survival. But calculating how to handle the weight of care not only will keep you out of the ocean where the shark swims, but will give you the wisdom to know the danger of attempting to swim where danger lies. So the conclusion of caring is wisdom. A caring person is wise, and wisdom is strength.

A person who cares is both wise and strong. The world exists because of caring people. As long as the world turns, there will be great opportunities to care. When people are born, they need care. Survivals of deceased love ones need care. People who do not have enough money to survive need care. People who are in torn relationships need care. People who fail at things after they have tried hard need care. People who are injured or get sick need care. People who get old need care. Lost, sick, or injured animals need care. Plants and flowers need care. Houses need care. Lawns and gardens need care. Almost all things need care, which leads us to believe that caring is very important. Caring has a guest list that includes the humblest to the noblest of people. In one way or other, we all will be on that list.

Proof of genuine, sincere care is not seen in the outward act, but in the action of the heart. Granted, money or selfish reasons can motivate the act of caring, and the character may exclude any form of gratitude. Some people want money for everything they do. Some people want applause for the things they do. Then there are those people who do things because they really do care, and their heartfelt actions speak louder than words. These caring people are the ones who carry the weight of the world on their shoulders. They are the ones that dry tears, bandages wounds, and bring comfort. They are not the glamorous people. They do not shine with the glitter of diamonds and gold because their hands are always dirty. They accept the back row seats, because that is where the hurting people are seated. They will eat last, because, as caring people, suffering is just part of who they are.

We are not born with the propensity to care. When we come into this world, all the attention is given to us until we are out of the egocentric stage of life. We are born with the innate ability to care, but until we are trained how to do so, this character trait lies dormant. Once the caring quality is brought to the surface, we will start to put others' needs before our own wants. If you watch children in their preschool years playing together, you will quickly see the selfish, independent, super-egotistical, possessive attitude arise when they cannot have someone else's toys. But, if the caring nature is cultivated through training by the parents or caregivers, that child will began sharing with other kids. Sharing will create an attitude of caring. Children that share will gain friendship with other children. Ultimately, friendship will develop into children learning the art of caring. As I stated earlier, what a person learns in his or her character during the tender ages will stick with him or her long into adulthood. Because we are frail creatures, unpredictable when faced with contrary situations, it is possible for us to be persuaded to change from the good that has been deposited in our human caring system.

No parent or caregiver should allow their children to continue a relationship with people who teach contrary to having a caring attitude. If they are not taught to care for someone and something, they become selfish, conceited, or possibly prejudiced. Caring is a sister to love. If they do not care, they will dislike. Dislike can lead to hatred. Hatred has no friends. Caring is universal with myriad of friends. It is not limited to family or country, church or temple. It is for everybody and everything. This is why the character of true Christianity is America's foundation; it cares for all people in all situations. It breathes *dedication.*

AMERICANS THAT CARED

Regardless of our ethnicities, Americans help Americans and other nationalities. In every success story there are people and persons in the background pushing individuals toward their personal goals. Generally it is not people directly related to the person. People who are related to us should invest positive things so the returns will glorify the family. It is only fair for the ones who have jumped over the hurdle of life to acknowledge and give due praise to others that had positive influences in their life. I want to give praise to some of the people who were not related to me while I was in my adolescent developmental stage of life. Especially to the Whites, so the Blacks will know that every white person is not out there to kill or imprison you. Martin Luther King Jr. stated that we should judge a person by the contents of his or her character. You cannot put everybody in the same boat. Most black people mean well. Most white people mean well. Some people, both Black and White, are going to act according to their father, the devil.

While I cannot mention everyone, I would like to mention a few.

Mrs. Blanche Coger
Coach Richard Gilliam
Mrs. Anne Parker
Mrs. Barbara BelIsles

A BLACK AMERICAN WOMAN
WHO TOUCHED MY LIFE

Blanche Coger was a high school teacher in Montevallo, Alabama. She taught at Prentice High School before the integration. She taught history and specialized in the Constitution of the United States of America. After 1967, when the black and white schools integrated, the Shelby County Board of Education sent her and other teachers to different schools. Mrs. Coger was sent to Montevallo Junior High School, where she continued to teach history.

My knowledge of Mrs. Coger prior to 1973, comes from Mrs. Minnie Pearl White of Montevallo. Above everything we may know of Mrs. Coger, Mrs. White wants us to know that she loved people and put determination in all her students to excel in life.

Mrs. Blanche Coger was of average height and stout. She was tough and did not put up with anyone's foolishness. She was very concerned about her students and made it her business that they learned the material she assigned. Most of her students could recite the Bill of Rights, the beginning of The Declaration of Independence, and the Preamble to the Constitution. She had a teaching style like none of her fellow teachers.

From one generation to the next, she put fear in her students. She understood the different learning levels and abilities of each student, but no matter what learning level each student had, she expected each one to learn. She did not accept excuses from the brightest to the least. She expected her students to properly enunciate their words so they would be able to communicate to others what they had learned. She communicated to her students the reason they needed to express themselves clearly, which was to function and get ahead in society.

In Prentice High School, she taught the students about where they came from and where they were going. It was her belief that the color of our skin could be a hindrance, or, on the other hand, we could use our education and ability to communicate, thereby getting ahead in life. She lived in the time when dark skin color was the "enemy." She never spoke against the majority; she just taught the Blacks that they could not get ahead and be respected as human beings without being knowledgeable, effective communicators.

In 1973, I had my first encounter with this great black American woman. She was my eighth grade history teacher. The one thing she told us was that we came to school to learn, and learn we would. While she was talking to the class and to each student, we all sensed this presence of strength and control that rested with her. Her voice was heavy, and her words were convincing. When she smiled occasionally, we could see the gap in her front teeth, which was her trademark. When she smiled, it meant she was very serious. Her words were crisp and clear; every syllable could be understood. Her words penetrated our very being until the white students no longer saw her as this big black lady. They saw her as a teacher and revered her as much as the black students who had known her for years.

My proudest moment in her class was the time I recited the Preamble and the Bill of Rights. In her class I learned things about American history that stick with me today: who I am and where I am going. She would personally say to me, "Rutledge, do you know why I'm making you learn this stuff?" I would admit, "No ma'am." She would say, "Because you are an American. You are just like all these white kids. You must know your rights if you expect to succeed. The only thing that makes you equal, other than the Bible, is this Constitution. I want you to know it." She would tell me to stay out of trouble because I had a bright future ahead of me.

I will never forget the day she scolded me for failing a test. She gave me my paper, pulled me up out of my seat, literally dragged me out into the hallway, took a measuring ruler, and hit my hand. Then she said to me, "Don't you ever fail another test in my class. I am not here just to be here. You can't get anywhere by failing."

From that day until I went into the ninth grade, I passed all the tests in her class. She would tell us to do at least two book reports a year. She made me do mine on black leaders that came out of slavery, people like Harriet Tubman, Fredrick Douglass, George Washington Carver, W.E.B. Dubois, and others. The history of these people taught me that my skin color did not determine my future. Mrs. Coger was right. The people that did not like my skin color could not stop me from being equal with them, if I knew my rights.

She understood the spirit of the Constitution above the letter of it. Her understanding of it transcended the teachers I had in high school. She was free and equal. She could prove it. She had a law that made her free and equal. She wanted to share that with those who needed it. Even if she had to force it in our brains, she knew we must have it. Our life in society depended on it.

She walked among all the people with grace and integrity. I never will forget that afternoon I slapped one of my friends around for hitting another friend of mine. She heard about the incident and rushed to my homeroom class. She asked the teacher if she could speak to me. I had no knowledge of what was coming down. When I left the room, she snatched me to the side and said, "Rutledge, you are a special child. I am expecting a lot from you. I want you to understand that you have to be strong in this life, but don't you ever think you are better than anybody else. I am ashamed of you. I better never hear talk of you fighting or getting into trouble again. Do you understand me?" With tears streaming from my eyes, and running down my cheeks, I said, "Yes, ma'am." That scared the daylights out of me. Then she said, "Now you go and apologize to that person."

Mrs. Coger gave me more than the letter of the Constitution; she taught me the spirit of it. Through her I learned to value the spirit of a thing. Knowing your rights and staying out of trouble, along with knowing who you are, are the keys to successful living. Because of Mrs. Blanche Coger, I am strong. I can look at everyone as equals. I understand the social advantage of being able to communicate effectively. Mrs. Coger has been deceased for many years now, but her memory lives on through many of the ones she taught.

A Black American Man Who Touched My Life

After Almont Elementary School integrated with Montevallo Elementary School, I met my sixth grade gym teacher, Mr. Arthur Greenlea. Mr. Greenlea understood youth and its energy. For many of the Blacks and Whites, this was their first time interacting on this social scale of life; therefore, we had some problems adjusting to each other. Mr. Greenlea, from my observation, never treated the Whites or the Blacks any differently. He was the catalyst to destroying the division between us. He would always mix us up in all the sporting actives. The white males were paired with the Blacks so that we could learn how to work together.

I can remember several times during our bonding period, when we would have our black and white skirmishes, Mr. Greenlea would make each group feel that it was their fault, and then scold us on top of that. One day while playing dodge ball, Ronnie Booth and another one of his friends were playing on the floor, ignoring what was going on. I walked over and banged him in the head with the ball. He jumped up, and we got into a fight. Mr. Greenlea took us into the back office where he preceded to lecture us about the importance of collaboration. Ronnie was like the leader of the Whites, and I was that to the Blacks. Mr. Greenlea shared that fact with both of us and stated that we were the keys to future harmony. Ronnie and I bought into it and became the best of friends.

That little talk, without further punishment, stopped many problems from occurring. He, being a black man, never came behind Ronnie's back to say anything differently than what he stated in that back office. He had wisdom. After leaving middle school, I remember Mr. Greenlea approaching one of my high school coaches while I was in the weight room. He told him these words that I will never forget: "Coach, you see this young man? He is dedicated to whatever you want him to do. You don't have to worry about him. He will be there for you." Those words keep echoing in my life up to this day. They have helped me work through difficult situations that people have told me to get out of. His words have made me tough, so that I will not give up so easily. The positive reinforcement I received from this man helped me to appreciate others as human beings. Like Mrs. Blanche Coger, Mr. Greenlea showed me that being Black did not mean hating white people.

A WHITE AMERICAN MAN WHO TOUCHED MY LIFE

After leaving Montevallo Middle School, I met Coach Richard Gilliam during the summer baseball league. I was the starting pitcher for the summer league in Montevallo. He was the umpire, and he had become the athletic director of Montevallo High School. Many of us believed that his eyesight was bad. For example, I was pitching a pretty good game, but around the fifth inning he started calling some strikes as balls. It probably was my fatigue, but I blamed his eyesight. I was mad and said words I should not have said. He stopped me right in my tracks and yelled to me from behind the catcher, "Big-um, what did you say? If you expect to play one game of sports for this school after this day, you'd better run ten laps around this baseball field." He was not joking, and I wanted to continue playing. He stayed after the game and stood there until I had run ten complete laps. He said to me afterward, "Don't you ever let me hear anything like that come out of your mouth again." Coach said to me some years later that he was glad I decided to run those laps, because he felt I was a good talent and he did not want to lose any of us that had talent.

That day changed my life forever. It made me appreciate that a white man could care so much about me. I had seen and heard all the negative things a person could see about a white man. At that moment I found a real man: not White or Black, but a real man.

Coach was a strict Baptist Christian. He commanded respect from players and coaches alike. He was a man of great integrity. He would sit down with each of us and talk about the goodness of God. We pretended we knew God, so when we were with him we acted the part of a Christian. But as soon as the cat was away the mice would play. Most of us were such young hypocrites. We did not know any better because that is what we learned in the local churches. Coach started taking me to the Christian Fellowship meetings where I met many professional athletes. I heard great stories of failures and successes. I heard these great athletes tell their stories of how God was helping them through the trials of life and how their faith was growing every day. I saw the so-called Christians at those meetings say one thing in the meeting but live another life on television. But Coach Gilliam remained the same—no hypocrisy in this man. He was who he said he was. I grew up Baptist; the other Baptists I knew talked about God on Sunday and lived for the devil the remaining six days. But Coach, he was real. He was my example. I love him for what he deposited in my life.

He spent countless hours away from his family to do his job as a coach and mentor. (Thank God for his understanding wife, Ola Faye Gilliam.) Every grading period he would check our report cards to make sure we were passing our classes. Many times he would come to our house, pick us up for practice, and take us home after practice. The school we attended was small, and most of us had to play the major three sports, but we did not care as long as we were playing directly or indirectly for Coach Gilliam.

In the 1970s we had to play many schools in Alabama that had not become aware of the fact that black people were also humans. Coach Gilliam never once displayed to me that his coaching covered up his prejudice; I never saw any prejudice or partiality in Coach. In fact, many times when the white students, umpires, coaches, and athletes would turn on us, he was right there to defend his players.

One sad incident happened in a place called Greenville (I think that was the city), Alabama. We were playing their baseball team. My cousin Percy Brown was pitching. He was striking out everyone that came to the plate. The white umpire saw that all hope of his team winning was lost. To help them out he started calling balls on all of Percy's pitches. Coach Gilliam approached the umpire in a godly manner. He went back to the bench, but the umpire kept calling the game the same way. Coach Gilliam pulled us off the field. We packed up our gear, but before we headed home, he apologized and spoke plainly about the matter. He stated it was prejudice against us because Percy was black and the white players could not hit his pitches. One thing he said to us in the short meeting will live with me forever: "If they had tried to harm us in any way, I would have been the first one to fight back." His stock rose with me on that day and forever.

Along with the loving care of my mother, Coach gave me hope. He would not let me quit, even though I was not the strongest or fastest athlete. He kept pushing me to be the best I could be with the talent I had. He kept me in check, and I let him do so. I so much appreciate this godly man. Black and white Americans must see people as people. There are some Whites that do not want to hear a black person, and there are some Blacks that do not want to hear a white person. However, everyone should have something good that they can deposit into someone else's life. Let us not be belligerent in thinking that because of the color of a person's skin they will not be able to help us.

A White American Woman Who Touched My life

In Montevallo High School we had some wonderful teachers. Granted, I saw some things I did not like in some of the white teachers and students, which I addressed. Because of the harsh treatment that the older generation of Blacks had to go through, we were told, "These white folks do not care a thing about you." As with everything in life, that was partially true. However, besides Coach Gilliam I had another white teacher that actually cared for me. In fact I believe I was one of her favorites. Her name was Mrs. Anne Parker. She would constantly tell me that I had what it took to make it in life. She would always make sure that my homework was completed. She would look in my eyes to see if I understood what she was talking about. Many times after the bell rang, she would stop me before I left the classroom just to put that little encouragement into me that students sometimes need.

I remember one assignment she gave us in art class. Each student had to create something much different from the other. I took my jean jacket and drew a lion on the back of it. I embroidered a beautiful image of a lion with a large mane on it. She said to me, "I know yours will look good, because you always do your best." The jacket turned out very beautiful. It took a lot of hard work, but who cares; her initial encouragement made me work through all the setbacks.

As graduation from high school loomed, I remember she made me pass some of my final exams with 100s. She pushed me because she cared for me. She never gained anything from the encouragement she gave to me. She did not do it to be seen or paid by me in the future. She did it because she cared. I can never forget that wonderful woman. My high school friend, Jan Lovelady, reminds me of this wonderful woman; she places all of her students in the human category.

ANOTHER BLACK AMERICAN WOMAN WHO TOUCHED MY LIFE

Mrs. Barbara Belisle taught English and Literature while I was at high school. We had fun in her class. She would give us "plenty of line" to be students but would reel us in when it was necessary. She was a teacher first and a pal when it counted.

Teachers today cannot get away with the things the teachers in my day could. Mrs. Belisle gave us liberty to express our personality in class as long as we were not rude or obscene. When we got out of control, she would use those strong, harsh, but loving words, "You ignoramuses. You people act like wild beasts. Frank and James sit down and shut up. You girls with your little silly giggle shut up." There were times when she would make students stand in the corner of the classroom. She would make me recite whatever recitations we were working on until I recited them correctly. Her classes were so much fun.

I remember one time in class her son Billy was acting out of order. She made him leave the class. "Billy," she said, "get out of my class." Billy protested, "Maaaa." She replied, "I'm not Ma, my name is Mrs. Belisle" Then she used that word we loved so much: "You ignoramuses." That day she put about six of us out of class. The next day everything was back to normal.

I loved those little chats she and I would have at the close of my high school days. "Frank," she would say to me, "you are going to make it. Just keep doing what you are doing. Don't get into trouble and don't follow the crowd that's not interested in succeeding in life." I knew she cared for me as a student and as a person. In our many little talks she never tried to convince me that I had to hate white people in order to be successful in life. I am sure she had been discriminated against, but I never saw her hold a grudge against the Whites. She passed this strength on to me. I do not have to hate to succeed.

In her own loving, sometimes demeaning, strong, non-prejudicial, witty ways she affected most of us positively. We laughed at her derogatory characterization of us, because we knew she never meant a word of it. Sometimes she would laugh at herself while trying to be strong against us. James Reed and I would just sit back and laugh. But I also knew when to sit back and not laugh. I appreciate her guidance in the early and latter stages of my development as a teenager. She was an excellent influence to keep youths from developing prejudice in their hearts.

Some key people in my life told me not to trust white people and tried to make me hate them. Therefore, I am so glad God put Mrs. Coger, Mr. Greenlea, Coach Gilliam, Mrs. Parker, and Mrs. BelIsles in my life at the times when He did. These people played a key part in developing my character while growing up in Alabama. Each and every one of us needs someone like these people in our lives.

I honestly have no prejudices against people as a result of the history of racial discrimination against black Americans. I know that success and wealth are based on holistic freedom. I also know that people can accumulate wealth and at the same time have prejudice in their heart, but they will never have inward peace. Fear of what they project as evil will cause them to start judging even those that are similar to them. From middle school to high school to the military to joining the church and reentering the civilian community, the freedom I have in my heart and spirit to associate with people of different colors and to forgive the past is a direct result of the love of God and the teaching of the five persons I mentioned earlier. I had some extremely good influences in my life that helped shaped my understanding of diversity in America. These positive influences helped me to disbelieve the following things: white folks are no good; I cannot trust them; the white man is keeping me down; the white man will never change.

If I fellowship with people who hate other people, I am going to be held back spiritually, emotionally, and mentally. Fellowshiping with people of hateful character will always have you looking over your shoulder. No one can be successful in life while looking back over his or her shoulder each minute of the day. This is the reason the ex-slaves had such a difficult life after the emancipation. The enemy was on their heels constantly trying to stop their progress and destroy them. The fear of being killed or raped or tortured prevented many of the ex-slaves—who could have been successful—from venturing too far from their slave mentality, so they congested communities and villages. This history of abuse can cause black people to look in the past and be hindered from progressing in the future, or they can become successful in the future by not allowing the past to hinder them.

CHAPTER 18
WE ARE EQUAL

THE POOR ARE IN EVERY COUNTRY

The term *poor* denotes lowly financial status. America has many poor people, but regardless of this status they are equal. Because of slavery and the continuous defying of the law by white corporate businesses, black Americans as a people made much less money than the average majority household in America. After the Civil Rights movement in the sixties (the era that proved to be the straw that caused the camel to drag its belly on the ground), many black Americans enjoyed many more opportunities to prosper than at any time in the history of this country. For example, only a few free black Africans became rich during the time of slavery. These were exceptions to the rule.

Jesus' statement regarding having the poor with us always was a definitive truth. It was a reality during His time and shall be as long as civilization exists. Throughout history, in every age and in every country, poor people were there. The greater part of the world's population was, is, and will be poor. There will always be poor people from birth to the grave. The sad and unfortunate truth about people's financial possessions is that they cannot take it with them beyond the grave. Many wealthy people die poor because they spend all their assets trying to get well during the course of a serious illness. Many have to spend down their assets to live on the Medicaid programs. Now and forever, being poor is part of what we are, who we are, and what we will become. But while we are alive, everyone is not going to be poor, and everyone is not going to be rich.

Some people were financially great while they were alive, but we that are still living are greater than they are at the moment. But when we die, we will all be financially equal: broke and poor. All of us will have nothing. Whether our assets add up to two billion or fifteen cents, after we die the grave makes us equal. The end result of our wealth and riches is vanity. (See Ecclesiastes 1:1-2.) Here are some additional reasons why people will likely be poor:

- People that are born with physical disabilities
- People in remote parts of the country
- People that use illegal drugs
- People that are institutionalized
- Children born to parents on Welfare
- Children born in the slums
- People who had their life savings invested in the stock market before it crashed
- People who lose their jobs when the entire country is facing financial difficulties
- People that work hard everyday for minimum wage
- People with mental disabilities

Being poor is not shameful; however, it does present struggles and hardships for daily living based in part on the geographical area in which the poor people live. The poor that live in the city have a much harder time coping with the lack of daily substances than those that live in rural or farming areas. Being poor and living in the city does not necessarily mean that the people are in poverty. Poverty can be a defeated state of mind. Poverty can also be the result of living in a country that is destitute economically. Sociologists want you to have only one view of poverty: theirs. Countries ravished by AIDS and in poverty should not be compared with the status of a person that makes $15,000 a year and lives a moral, decent life.

Contrary to some, many poor people live a decent lifestyle and become very successful. They pay their bills, they work, they keep their houses clean, and their children are raised to be decent and respectful citizens. Contrary to some sociological studies, every poor person is not an alcoholic or a drug addict or a mental patient. Being poor does not mean you are a bad person. *Poverty*, on the other hand, is a bad thing. The following reasons are why many poor people fall into poverty:

- They are not good stewards of their money.
- They develop a defeatist mentality.
- They turn to intoxicating substances.
- They accept the stereotypical, demographical lie that tells people where they are financially, socially, and educationally will be where they will remain. (Note: You, who were born into a poor situation, do not have to remain in that situation. If, for whatever reason life does not afford you the income to become middle class or rich, your character should always tell others that you are rich.)
- They live in a country where the government will not allow the God of blessings to be praised.

Many so-called Black Leaders are trying to persuade Blacks that the White man is still suppressing them. They are trying to instill hate instead of instilling confidence to become successful by doing what it really takes to have a chance at enjoying the wealth of this nation. They quote the lack of programs by the current president to help black people get ahead, as though any program will help, except for the program established by God. God's program (paraphrased) states, "Serve Him. Stop having babies outside of marriage. Get off your lazy butts and go find a job. Pay your tithes, give to the needy, and God will open the windows of heaven and shower blessings on you."

We need to work regardless of the type of job. Fast food restaurants, local grocery stores, summer jobs with the city, or even gas station attendants are not run-of-the-mill jobs; they are decent jobs. They will help you get through college so that after you earn your degree you will be able to get a higher-paying job. These jobs will help you pay your household bills.

It is better to work in these places than to sell drugs, steal, or sell your body. These negative things often reduce a person to slavery. But working at honest jobs will give you honest money, while these lowlife jobs will destroy you for the rest of your life. The spirit of the flag does not promote this lowlife type of lifestyle. Contrariwise, the flag offers help if you want to start a better life. To blame the government or any other ethnic group for character downfall is asinine and selfish.

We must have an inward drive to do the right things if we are to succeed in this wealthy country. We must get a good education. We must live according to the law. We must go to work. We must give back to help those in need.

Every citizen must strive to be the best he or she can be. No one should expect handouts. I watched my mother manage the little she had. Through her sacrifices, she taught me a very valuable lesson: never expect anyone to support me. The character I developed as a result of paying attention to her lifestyle gave me the fortitude to work hard in every aspect of life. In order to have the best in life, I would have to earn my way with little help along the way. She showed me how to be happy on a poor person's income. Many people have a sad view of life; they believe that if they are not rich then life is not fair. Who told you that you would not have to go through tough times? Everyone is saying, why me? I say, why not you? Who owes you anything after you become an adult? Just because you graduated from college does not mean corporate America owes you a job. Just because your forefathers were slaves does not mean the government owes you reparations. Just because you are white does not mean you are going to walk in an office and be assigned a high-paying job or any job. This life is about earning your way. Do not say God is unfair because you do not have what you think you should have.

People that start out poor can become rich. Nothing is impossible when you are under the banner of "Old Glory." But if a person does not have a financially rich status, it should not prevent him or her from becoming spiritually rich. Remember that the poor made it possible for the Statue of Liberty to be erected. I have been around the poor all my life. I know success stories of poor people becoming rich while remaining financially poor. These people are hard-working, and they do not consider themselves poor because they do not have a defeatist attitude. Being poor financially does not make you the degradation of the world.

We black Americans have come too far not to succeed in life. This country has much to offer. It is mine. God made it for me. I shall salute it. If the black Africans had not come to this country, they would not have been showcased as great inventors and orators. While in slavery and under the pressures of Jim Crow laws, Blacks were force to show they were more than slaves. The world has been blessed because of the great inventions of the black African slaves and the black Americans. This would have never happen if we had not come to this country.

America gave us the opportunity to be great. Let me say to the entire black American population, I understand the pain many have endured. This statement is by no means an attempt to ignore the past or the present struggles. But when we look at the full scope of the prosperity of the Blacks in other countries, we are much more prosperous in America than our kinsmen according to the flesh. Now put up your gun, go back in the house, and continue reading this book.

Many Black American leaders are still preaching poverty and suppression. When one black movie star (who shall remain nameless) was asked a question concerning suppression in America, and if he was better off now, he replied, "Nothing has changed." Yet this person is making million of dollars per movie, most of it derived from white moviegoers. This answer came from a very successful person with a defeatist attitude.

It is a shame for these men and women who enjoy the wealth of this nation to mold the thinking of their constituents into defeatist knuckleheads. If we take a look around us, we will see that a great many of us are not as bad off as the scenarios black and white leaders tend to broadcast. Much of the media show the economical advancement of the black Americans: Jet, *Ebony*, DiversityInc, Worldwide Success Guide, Black Career Women, Essence, *The Black Business Journal, The Network Journal* magazine, *Black Entertainment* magazine, *The Atlanta Tribune, Black Press* magazine, Vibe, BET, Fox television, Disney, and many others. You will be surprised at the amount of money black Americans are making (rightly deserved) in the religious, business, political, and the sports worlds. However, money is not everything; leadership is. These men and women that are mentioned in the media worked hard to get where they are. This generation should observe the past and current successes and realize the great opportunities that await them. A good education can put you in position for great achievements. Do not allow people that cannot get over their own hurts to stop you from obtaining what is rightfully given to you by God and the Constitution of the United States. If we black Americans want to go forward, we must look back at the successes of our forefathers. The stripes on their backs should motivate us to receive stripes on our graduation robe sleeves!

The slaves were poor by force, but God heard their prayers, and their posterities are blessed today because of it. Look around you black Americans: when you see black men and women signing contracts worth million of dollars, this should let you know that we are not as poor as some Blacks and Whites make us out to be. This is what the flag is all about. As I stated earlier, there are more poor Blacks than rich Blacks. Also, there are more poor

Whites than rich Whites. Look at the Indian community. How many on the reservation are rich? Not many. They deserve all the riches this government can give. But, the government is not here to make people rich. Most of us have the same opportunities. If some do not get there, it will be okay. Live within your means. Remember that being poor may be more of a mental state than an economical one.

WHAT DO YOU SEE IN THE MIRROR?

The Bible states that when a man beholds himself in a mirror and then walks away, he immediately forgets what type of man he is. As a citizen of this country, what do you see when you look in the mirror? Do you see an American, or an individual white or black person, or a Jew, or a Muslim who thinks your view of what Americans ought to be is hidden behind what your eyes see in the mirror? (All other ethnic groups and religions are considered with the groups mentioned above.)

When Americans look in the mirror, they should perpetually see the flag that represents them. After we leave the mirror, we should see everyone in this manner. The flag is the mirror; it is red, white, and blue, with fifty stars and thirteen stripes. It is the citizens of the United States of America. No one person or ethnic group owns the rights to the liberty and justice that were granted to all citizens of this country. No one is greater than the flag. Only prejudice can keep you from seeing the red, white and blue, but your prejudices do not make void the truth.

The flag in the mirror tells all that look in it that even though the object may be black, white, brown, red, yellow, male, female, tall, short, fat, or skinny, the flag will never change. With this understanding, one should have the strength to pursue the life of happiness in this land that offers liberty to all. If someone attempts to take your rights from you, you must fight. It is better to fight for your rights than to sit passively and blame others. No person knowingly should treat you unjustly and get away with it. There is much injustice in the world, even in this great country. For anyone to say otherwise would be to speak as a fool. The great thing about this country is that you have the flag. As long as your sight remains, you will see the flag. Even if you are blind, you can still see those colors. The flag is so powerful that it causes a blind person to see its image in the mirror. Only when you are overtaken with destructive habits can you become blinded so you cannot enjoy the benefits of the flag.

When people enter into the egotistical, self-serving, internalized, prejudicial, conceited tunnel vision of hatred, they are blind to what the flag has given others in this country. They also jeopardize their own freedom. The good thing about understanding your rights is that you may have to offend the ones who are trying to stop you from having those rights. No one is greater than the flag; therefore, it may be necessary to offend those in authority who act contrary to the purpose of the flag. If they cannot see you as equal with them, then they are blind to the image in the mirror. The power of proper judicial enforcement for justice will cause individuals, corporations, and law enforcement to look at you through the flag.

Teachers, policemen, lawyers, bankers, and employers, which are part of civil community, must be cognizant of the purpose of the flag or else risk the punishment of the same. The flag that allows liberty is the same flag that imprisons and punishes people for violating the law it represents. The United States government, for the most part, has stopped being hypocritical regarding justice. I believe that the government is striving to improve its relationship with all of it citizens. Whether millionaire black people think so or not, there have been great changes. The people of America must put fear in those that will overlook the image in the mirror. The fastest way to make people respect the image in the mirror is by lawsuits. We are lawsuit-happy; the entire nation is lawsuit-happy. Take Enron and other companies, for example. The government went after Enron with a lawsuit, because lawsuits bring fear and make people comply. The whole attitude behind lawsuits is to make people and companies walk the walk of equity. Money is not the total purpose. The flag says we are one in the eyes of the law, and lawsuits say, "You messed up and knew it, so I'm going to make you walk the walk." There are no black Americans, no white Americans, no Irish Americans, no Italian Americans and so forth, when it comes to the law that the flag represents. When you look in the mirror, you will only see the flag staring back at you.

The best way to speed up equality for all Americans is for white lawyers to take discrimination cases and process them for court hearing. If enough cases are won, I guarantee you that corporations will start looking at their hiring practices. Banks will start looking at their lending practices. Realtors will start looking at what houses they neglect to show the potential homebuyer. It is okay if we have a billion lawsuits a year. You may ask, "Isn't that a slippery slope?" It may be but you do not have to worry about it if you are not discriminating. Lawsuits are legal.

The Talk around the Table

Every country has a minority, which is a smaller group of people among the general population of a country. The minority is the group that is least respected, and they are the ones that have fewer privileges. Whether this is bad or considered an attitude of indifference, this is the way we humans treat each other. As the horse said in the movie *Babe*, "The way things are, are the way things are." The world is full of segregation and prejudice. Segregation and prejudice are carried from generation to generation until someone puts the ax to the root of the tree. Most of the time prejudicial attitudes stem from the dinner table. Children will repeat what they hear.

The story goes that two women who attended the same church were friends. One woman had a little daughter about eight years old. When the mother of the child was at home talking to her friends, the little girl played but listened to the adult conversations. After a Sunday morning church service, the little girl went to the beloved friend and jumped in her arms, as she had always done in the past. However, this time the little girl stared at the beloved friend with bewilderment. The woman said to the little girl, "Baby, what's the matter?" The little girl said, "I'm looking at your face because my mother said you had *two* faces."

In some countries political and religious groups have mercy on whom they shall, but it is not so in America. The political practices in this country are governed by the Judeo-Christian belief that all men are created equal; therefore, they should be treated equally. The Constitution provides the letter of the law that tells all how to respect the common welfare of each citizen and stranger, and the federal government enforces that law. But, it is up to adult family members to enforce the great law of morality.

Our oldest son attended a private Christian school prior to entering the tenth grade, at which time my wife and I allowed him to transfer to public school. He was the first black American child for many years at the Christian school. He had white and black friends in the city. From his parents' mouths he had never heard derogatory statements about white or black people. While at the Christian school most of his friends were white, but regardless of his friendly white associations, when he went to public school, he picked up derogatory names for Whites, Hispanics, Blacks, and others. In my house we do not tolerate calling people derogatory names. We preach the love of Christ to our children. What if we sat at the dinner table and spoke negatively about other ethnic groups? He would think the same thing about us as he did about the other hypocrites. It is hard enough making our children respect us with the many flaws we parents have, without adding hypocrisy to the list. As the Bible states, "A little leaven leavens the whole lump" (I Corinthians 5:6). In other words, if you are prejudiced, you will never be able to hide it; it will rise in front of your children.

The reason most children say so-called foolish things about other children is the result of dinner table conversations. Have you ever been around a group of children playing together and one of them says something racial that embarrasses the mother and father? Someone would say, "Children say the darndest things." Yes they do, but most of the time they get it from—yes, you guessed it—the sweet, dark-hearted, dear parents. If you are insecure about yourself and use N-, C-, H-, and other words, how can you expect your children not to do likewise? The apple does not fall too far from the tree, especially if the tree is located on flat, level ground. Let us hope when the apple does fall that some secure person will pick it up, clean it off, and give it a new start in life. I hope that the person who has been changed will rebuke their friends and loved ones for making negative statement about others.

My mother had a hard time forgiving white people. She grew up in the era and an area where the Whites treated the Blacks the same as slaves. My mother would clean the houses of some of the so-called rich white people, but her "wages" were clothes or food. One day she brought home by mistake a KKK suit from the home of one of my father's bosses. I did not know what it was, so I wore it at Halloween. These people pretended to care about her, but once her back was turned, they mocked her. She did not trust any white person because of the way she had been treated. At times I confronted her about her feelings toward all white people. She would say to me, "Son, just pray for me." She later changed but reserved judgment. If we are Christians and Americans, we must learn to forgive the past. Remember that what you say in front of your children around the table will be repeated when you least expect it.

CHAPTER 19
FORGIVE THE PAST?

American textbooks are written by people who are afraid of their own shadows. These authors are trying to hide valuable truths from a generation of Americans in the hope that we will believe that this country is great only because of the Europeans. Many black writers have undertaken the task of broadcasting the wonderful things that former black African slaves and black Americans have contributed to this country. May all Americans find in the following accomplishments a wealth of pride knowing that "Americans made it happen."

BLACK AMERICAN SUCCESS STORIES

1922—Aviator Bessie Coleman, who later refused to perform before segregated audiences in the South, staged the first public flight by an African American woman.

1923—Pianist and orchestrater Fletcher Henderson became a bandleader. His prestigious band advanced the careers of such black musicians as Louis Armstrong, Coleman Hawkins, and Roy Eldridge. Also during this year, Bessie Smith, discovered by pianist-composer Clarence Williams, made her first recording. She eventually became known as "Empress of the Blues."

1924—William DeHart Hubbard became the first black athlete to win an Olympic gold medal in an individual event at the Summer Games in Paris.

1930—Benjamin Oliver Davis Sr. became the first black colonel in the U. S. Army. He later oversaw race relations and the morale of black soldiers in World War II and became the first black general in 1940.

1937—Mahalia Jackson became one of the most celebrated gospel singers of her time. She traveled nationally and abroad, singing religious songs and refusing to sing jazz and the blues because of her faith in God. Her name was on secular as well as spiritual lips.

1936—Track-and-field athlete Jesse Owens won four gold medals in the Olympic games in Berlin. His victories derailed Adolf Hitler's intended use of the games as a show of Aryan supremacy.

1940—Hattie McDaniel became the first Black to receive an Oscar for her supporting role in *Gone with the Wind*.

1947—Jackie Robinson, the first black major league baseball player, earned the Rookie of the Year award. This award made the statement that he was better than all the white rookies he played with. Jackie helped integrate the Negro with the major leagues. Jackie Robinson played baseball for the Brooklyn Dodgers. In 1962, he was the first black inducted into the National Baseball Hall of Fame.

1948—Alice Coachman took gold in the high jump at the Olympic games in London. She was the first black woman to win Olympic gold and the only American woman that year to win.

1954—On May 17, the U. S. Supreme Court ruled unanimously in *Brown v. Board of Education of Topeka* that racial segregation in public schools violated the Fourteenth Amendment to the Constitution.

1955—Rosa Parks, secretary of the Montgomery, Alabama Chapter of the NAACP, refused to surrender her seat when ordered by a local bus driver, leading to the Montgomery bus boycott of 1955-56.

1955—Opera diva Leontyne Price triumphed in the title role of the National Broadcasting Company's *Tosca*, making her the first black to sing opera on television. That same year, singer and guitarist Chuck Berry traveled from St. Louis to Chicago, recording "Maybellene," an immediate sensation among teenagers. The hit helped to shape the evolution of rock and roll.

1964—Martin Luther King Jr. was the youngest person awarded the Nobel Peace Prize at the age of thirty-five. He was one of four great men of America's history alongside President George Washington, President Abraham Lincoln, and President John F. Kennedy.

1967—Thurgood Marshall was the first African American to be appointed to the U. S. Supreme Court.

1975—Lee Elder was the first Black to play in the Masters Tournament at Augusta, Georgia. In the same year, tennis player Arthur Ashe won the singles title at Wimbledon, becoming the first Black to win a major men's singles championship.

1983—Guion Steward Bluford Jr. was the first African American in space, and Vanessa Williams, Miss New York, was crowned the first black Miss America. On that day, my eyes well with tears when they announced that Vanessa was Miss America 1983.

1996—At the 1996 Olympic games in Atlanta, Georgia, sprinter Michael Johnson became the first man of any ethnic group to win gold medals in the 200-meter and the 400-meter races, setting a 200-meter world record of 19.32 seconds.

2002—Halley Berry became the first African American woman to be awarded an Oscar for best actress in a leading role. She won for her role in *Monster's Ball*. Denzel Washington won the Academy Award for best actor in a leading role for his part in *Training Day*. Tavis Smiley was the first African American to host his own signature program on NPR, and Michele Norris became the first black woman to regularly host an NPR newsmagazine.

1972—Shirley Chisholm was the first black woman that had enough faith and strength to run for the United State presidency.

Tiger Woods—From the media's perspective, Tiger was and is the greatest golf player alive. Because of him, non-golfers sit for hours and watch the best golfers become even better. His face and skin are black, but his greatness demands everyone's respect as an American.

Oprah Winfrey—First black female to host her own TV show that became the number one talk show for many years running.

Michael Jordan—The greatest basketball player that ever lived.

Colin Powell—First black male Secretary of State.

Florence Joyner—The most beautiful and fastest woman that has ever run in track-and-field.

Muhammad Ali—The greatest boxer in the history of boxing. The most electrifying personality of his time (White or Black). He was the people's champion.

Condoleezza Rice—First black female Secretary of State, who could easily become the nominee of the Republican Party for president of the United States in 2008.

Henry Aaron—Broke the major league homerun record held by the great Babe Ruth. Even while Whites threatened his life and Blacks urged him not to risk his life over a record, he played the game like Babe would have played it. He played to win games for his team.

SUCCESS FOR THE FUTURE!

The Indians, black Americans, and white Americans must forgive the past. Forgiveness is not for the victors, but for the victims. The victim is the one who has the scars and carries the mental, emotional, and spiritual burdens. In one way or the other we are all victims. Unforgiveness causes people to become victims. Unforgiveness creates more problems for the victims because it stops them from carrying out their daily routines. Most victims stop progressing because they want to row up a waterfall to take revenge on the person or thing that harmed them. Sometimes they use the court system to get back at the person that caused them the harm. While they may make progress in deterring acts of violence such as those perpetrated on them, they also go through many unnecessary physical, mental, emotional, and psychological hardships because they will not forgive.

If you do not forgive, you will start to hate. Hatred has no friends. When a heart starts to hate, no one is exempt from its wrath. Whether you are the father, mother, brother, sister, or relative of the ones that have the hatred in their hearts, you will become an enemy to them. In this life you will never forget what happened to you, but there must come a point and time when healing has to be accepted. As much as other people may try to bring you into that great banquet of forgiveness, it is up to you to get *yourself* there. Individually, we must come to closure with the hurts that have been inflicted upon us.

Forget the past, not by any means, but live in the present, by all means. Forgiveness is not putting your head in the sand and acting as if ignorance has vanished. We will never forget America's enslavement of the black Africans, Japan's bombing of Pearl Harbor, and the terrorist attack that brought down the Twin Towers on September 11, 2001. But if you do not forgive the ethnic groups that committed these crimes, you will treat everyone in the ethnic groups as criminals. Riches and wealth are more easily attained through forgiveness. The government will take care of the enemies.

We will never be able to correct the past or make people like us. Our purpose is not to get people to like us; our purpose is to be Americans. We must respect other people and respect ourselves as well. We cannot like ourselves if we do not take care of ourselves. I speak of taking care of ourselves individually (not of isolating ourselves, as some would have us do). We do not have to stop buying the products that others make. We do not have to stop depositing our money into banks where the president is not our color. Nor should black Americans stop shopping at stores where Blacks are not owners. But if the stores refuse to hire Blacks and other ethnic groups, we may need to consider not patronizing that company. If I may use the power of suggestion, I would strongly suggest you do not buy anything from any retailer that does not act American.

We black Americans must forgive the past before we can go forward emotionally. Today we are enjoying the prosperity that Whites have enjoyed for years. Even though we still have a few more miles to travel, we have a brighter future because we now understand the meaning of the flag. But we are still not healed from the emotional scars that have been caused by the past, and we are constantly reminded of that from those Blacks that are not secure in themselves. These scar-searchers hate Whites and want every black person to hate them as well. However, if you hate one person, you hate all people. Hatred infects the soul.

Blacks need to understand that every white American is not out to do them harm. There are some that are out to hurt you because of their evil hearts. The truth is that after man fell into sin, his nature went from love to hate. Now the sinful people, no matter what color they are, are out to harm people because this is part of their lifestyle. Even in countries where the people are of the same ethnicity, they fight against each other. So, it is not a color issue; it is a nature issue. Many people hide behind the doors of religion, professing to like other people in the name of God, but hating the fact that your skin is lighter or darker than theirs. These people will do whatever they can to whomever they can. But as the history of slavery taught us, you cannot keep good men and women down.

White Americans have to stop worrying about offending Black people. White Americans many times are afraid of using the ethnic word Black(s) when used in the proper context. I notice when I am having conversation with some of my white friends, they are hesitant to have an informative dialogue with me for fear they will offend me. Too many white Americans never get a chance to experience friendship with other ethnic groups because they subconsciously blame themselves for what happened in America's past. Or they listen to these so-called black leaders as they try to heap old crimes on innocent people. As a white American, if you do not move from that fear, you will never have a meaningful relationship with anyone from the other ethnic groups. In this free society many of us are cognitively in prison. This affects our perception of social happiness. You must forgive the past in order to have a brighter emotional future.

All the Europeans that held black Africans in slavery are dead. Most of the immediate ancestors of the slave masters are dead. The generation from the early 1900s is dead, dying, or very old. If you were not part of that system that tried to keep black Americans in bondage, you should not blame yourself for what happened in the past. And you do not have to apologize to every black person you meet. If you still have that ancient philosophy in your heart that Blacks are inferior to Whites, you must get rid of it because you are carrying a burden that causes cancer and other stress-related illness. You will become a victim of your own venom. Do not allow black people to make you feel that you are prejudiced just because you are white.

As I travel throughout the Northeast preaching at many churches, I get invited to preach at some local churches where the members are predominately white and some predominately black. And some are all white and all black. I love fellowshiping with the church in Ellsworth, Maine, where James Heard is the pastor. His congregation is all white. But they treat me as if I am white, and they treat me as if I am black; that is, they treat me like a human should be treated. I do not have to worry about offending them because we act toward each other in the manner in which God has created us to be. James Heard has a brother in Portsmouth, New Hampshire, named Larry Heard. He treats me just like his brother does. These white men do not put on fronts in my presence to make me believe they are something they are not. They do not live a fearful life always worrying about offending me as a black person. We can sit and have meaningful conversations about everything. The reason for this is that we see each other as persons and not colors. I have many white friends that are not "white" to me; when we see each other, we are colorblind.

Yet in some other churches where the membership is predominately white, when I walk in the sanctuary, I can sense that the people are still struggling with the idea that my skin is darker than theirs. The poor creatures; as they talk to me, it appears they are one breath away from cardiac arrest. They are still living in the old nature. I remembered attending an all-white church service where Bishop Eugene Redd was the preacher. He asked the congregation, "How many of you love black people?" Fearing that someone would say they were not good Christians, all hands went up. Then he asked, "How many of you would let your sons and daughters marry a black person?" Out of the hundred-plus that were there, maybe one or two hands went up. So for the hands that did not go up, you can imagine the conversations that took place around the dinner table.

I was sitting at dinner with a group of black church leaders in Connecticut. The discussion on interracial marriage came up. These dear, good, black Christian people stated that they did not want their sons and daughters to marry a white person. The poor creatures cannot let go of the past. It is a shame for these so-called God-forgiven black preachers to talk about white people the way they do and still profess that Christ is in their lives. These preachers use derogatory terms when describing all white people: "None of them are any good." "You can't trust any of them." At the same time, they invite white preachers to minister in their churches. These black preachers condemn Louis Farrakhan while internally holding to his ideologies regarding Whites. At least Mr. Farrakhan is honest.

It is time for total forgiveness in the name of the God we are preaching about. The God of Creation does not want us to hate anyone. If we hate others and say that we are a worshiper of God, we may as well change the capital G in God to a small g. We are only using the religious god as a crutch to do evil. How then can people blame their evil actions on a loving and gracious God whom they cannot see? We can blame our philosophy and evil ways on god, because this fake deity has no power to correct us. The true God through Jesus Christ demands that we forgive and not hate the creature that was created in His own image. We were made in the image of God. I believe that if we hate one another, we also hate God, because the command to love comes from God. The absolute truth is we do not have to accept people's immorality or applaud as they parade their sin through the streets, but we must respect them as people.

Many people want you to become one of them. For example, economics many times creates a culture in which friends are made because of like socioeconomic status. For the most part relationships like these are pretentious and phony. This fake "ethnic" group often represents insecurity, because everyone is trying to be like the next person to succeed in life. Unlike this phony group of people, ethnicity that is created by skin color cannot be changed. Therefore, you do not have to become one of them to enjoy them as people. Life is not about becoming one of them. We are who we are (human beings) without trying to change one another into who or what we are. We must learn to appreciate people for who they are in their ethnicity. Our skin color cannot change the fact that we are the same and different in so many ways. So why should we not have friends in the human race that are of a different ethnic group? Does not our flag represent oneness? Are we not all Americans? We will never forget the past; however, we are no longer slaves to the past. We now have a broader meaning of the flag, which teaches us that white people are not devils and black people are not slaves.

It is a shame for churches and universities to hold to the same old ideologies they embraced over three hundred years ago regarding ethnicities. Many of the well-known entities do not believe that a black man should marry a white woman, or a white man a black woman. They would not dare make the mistake of saying, "You cannot marry," because using the word "cannot" would indicate they have complete control over people and are forcing them not to marry. The word is too aggressive. The word "can" means ability. Everyone has the ability and freedom to marry whomever they choose. They want you to think you have your own will so they say, "Should not."

They dress up their prejudice by using the offspring as sacrifices.

1) You know the children will have a hard time growing up.
2) Your parents will reject both you and your family.
3) People will talk.

As condescending as this is to the one that is being spoken to, it reveals the ignorance of the one speaking. Think for one moment. How many of the above factors exist in all groups? Now, here is the most dangerous thing about the above statements: they are being taught by people in churches, religious institutions, and institutions of higher education. It would be better for all these churches and Christian schools to start preaching out of a comic magazine than to preach out of the Bible. The Bible condemns the very message they are trying to deliver. It is a shame for people who are supposed to have the God of the universe in their souls, to continue their foolish attack on the human race just because they have issues with themselves. They cannot see that we are one regardless of our color. Maybe the fight is not color at all. It may be economics. Do these people think that Blacks and Whites should not marry because Blacks are still living in the poverty of slavery?

The philosophy that some people hold to which states that different ethnic group should not intermarry has to be founded in some secret place. Think about this fact: The hatred for blacks did not start until the emancipation. The Declaration of Independence stated that all were created equal. The Emancipation Proclamation set the slaves free and gave them the same rights as previous citizens, thereby showing all were created equal. The slave owners and their friends were upset because their economy was ruined. Economics has separated more people than color ever did. When slaves could earn enough money, they could buy their freedom and gain status among the Whites. Everything was okay with this concept until there were no more slaves. Once all slaves were free, the thought of these once-enslaved people having opportunities of becoming equal was preposterous. In most instances, when people hate it is because they fear the abilities of others. If people are confident of their own ability, they will be able to trust it to get them through life, rather than wishing the downfall of others.

Educators and preachers state that their teaching about interracial marriage came from the Bible. However, this philosophy did not come from the Holy Bible. It may have come from another religious book, but not the Holy Bible. The Bible teaches that we are one. God commanded His people not to mingle with some of the neighboring people, or marry them because of their immorality, not because of their ethnicity. God never intended for false worship to be a part of His people's lives. If we have faith in Him, we should not mingle with fornicators, false worshipers, or those who commit gross immorality. God never planned for humans not to marry other humans because of the color of their skin. If ethnicity was the reason God commanded the Israelites not to mingle with the other nations, then He would not have allowed the following persons to have a part in their stellar history: Joseph's wife was from Egypt, Boaz's wife Ruth was from Moab, Balaam, a prophet of God was from Moab, Salmon's wife Rahab was from Jericho, Syrus was from Syria and many others from other nations. All of these "foreigners" played a big part in God's plan for His people. The apostle Paul who wrote so many New Testament books was a Jew who was a Roman citizen.

A mature adult man or woman should marry whomever they choose as long as they are morally compatible. When people and entities use the words "should not marry," they want you to act according to human dictates and philosophy. They put suggestions in your mind and tell you to obey, but at the same time they are leading you to believe that you have a choice after they have brainwashed you into believing Whites and Blacks are not to marry each other. This was old European thinking before the Quakers forced them to open and read the Bible. When people turn a blind eye and a deaf ear to the truth, no truth is safe from their will to corrupt it.

The saddest facts concerning this whole mess is that the so-called Christian churches and Christian universities still hold to the same foolish, unproven theory in this period of enlightenment. These entities should know that God created the male then took his rib and made a female. From my elementary knowledge of the anatomy, the rib has all the DNA traits of the person it came from.

Therefore, if the female was taken out of the male, then it would stand to reason that she would inherit all of his genes. If the whole creation is from these first two humans, it would not matter what color our skin is because we have the same DNA traits, and we are compatible for procreation. (See Genesis 2:22-23.) How can anyone come to a conclusion that there are separated races in the human family? We are males and females.

If the opponents of marriages between ethnic groups are right in concluding that it is devastating for America and other groups of the world to marry, then why is it that the commercials are showing little children saying "I'm Tiger Woods?" Tiger Woods married a white woman. Now, where are the opponents of "interracial marriages"? They are closed mouthed because of his financial status. Or, why is it that many white and black women and the sports world at large have Derrick Jeter posted everywhere? What about Jason Kidd? What about Thomas Jefferson's black offspring? What about Alex Haley? What about Bruce Lee's family? What about the Bibby family in basketball? What about my first cousin Robert Brazzel's children? What about the two sons of my brother Terry Rutledge? We call these people mixed. Mixed with what? Human blood and monkey's blood? We are so-o-o ignorant. Thank God for DNA tests. It finally has shut up many so-called supremacists and black power people, and has taken us back to our origin.

I am convinced that most baseball, basketball, and football owners wish they could clone some of these mixed athletes. I do not think the sporting world is fighting against interracial marriage because they have benefited by the athletic abilities of some of these individuals.

Should there be only pure Blacks and pure Whites in America? What are pure Blacks and pure Whites? What are we going to do with us that have so-called blood from different nationalities? Am I to tell my relatives that they are not real human beings? Does not our Constitution teach that we are created equal? Does the flag of the United States change color because it flies from an

Oriental family's home? I do not think so. For those who wish to eliminate what they call human mutts, it would be a wise gesture for them to do some serious genealogical research into there own family history. They will surprisingly discover that they are part of that mutt gang. With this historical finding, the attitude of eliminating human mutts will be derailed.

The absolute truth is that America represents what God intended for us to be: one big melting pot of people working together. God has blessed this country, and now He wants to bless us individually.

No One Is Better Than the Next Person

The apostle Paul stated, "And He has made from one blood every nation of men to dwell on all the face of the earth, and has determined their pre-appointed times and the boundaries of their dwellings, so that they should seek the Lord in the hope that they might grope for Him and find Him, though He is not far from each one of us; for in Him we live and move and have our being, as also some of your own poets have said, 'For we are also His offspring.' " (Acts 17:26-28)

The phrase, "all men are created equal," is more than a Declaration phrase; it is the truth. We all came through Adam and Eve who were created in the image of God: the first male and female. God gave them dominion over the works of His hands and gave them procreative abilities. Each one of us is born with a free will. That free will is never to be violated; however, because the nature of man is evil and cruel, he seeks to impose his self-centered, domineering ways upon others. God created government so that we could live in harmony with each other. In government there has to be those that exercise authority over others. The Bible states that righteousness exalts a nation but sin (crime) is a reproach to any people (Proverbs 14:34). When leaders rule in righteousness, they will be cognizant of the fact that their subjects are equal to them, because both were created in the image of God.

Throughout this book we are reminded that man migrated over the face of the earth and some gathered in their individual places. Cultures developed out of those gatherings. Kings, princes, queens, lords, peasants, herdsmen, blacksmiths, innkeepers, bankers, teachers, priests, philosophers, and such like are formed to make a nation and its communities. Within these cultures are good, indifferent, and bad people. No culture will ever be a paradise.

Paradise is where there is no crime. The Golden Rule is embedded in the hearts and minds of all citizens. Everyone is treated the same. Mercy and judgment are handed to everyone equally. Equality is not just a word in the dictionary; it is a practice entrusted to all citizens. However, paradise will not exist as long as the sons and daughters of Adam rule the world. There has only been one place that can truly be called Paradise: the Garden of Eden. Ironically, the devil visited it.

From early civilizations up to the present time, government is necessary to control people's bad habits. Human imperfection is center stage. Without a doubt, human imperfections produce crime. Here is the sad, debilitating knowledge about many who think that their ethnicity or culture is better than another's: they all have to build jails. The way to get beyond deceiving yourself into thinking your ethnic group is superior to another is to use the following rationale.

We all came from Adam and Eve. Adam and Eve were the same. Eve was bone of his bone and flesh of his flesh. Both were living souls with free wills. By using their free will, they decided to disobey God. Both failed God in a day. Therefore we are all the same.

If one person ever has broken one law that would cause him or her to be incarcerated, then it would stand to reason that the whole group is bad. The law of potentiality is based on sameness. From sameness we have the potential to do good or bad. Now, what stares us in the face is wrong habits. If one person has acted contrary to virtue, then all have the same potential because all came from the same stock. Adolph Hitler made the big mistake of trying to cleanse the world of all the evil that was in everyone outside of his chosen race. He finally accomplished part of his task when he committed suicide.

Every nation has within its confines a prison system to incarcerate those who do evil. People will eventually act out their potential to do wrong. Not one person can say they have never done wrong. Therefore not one person can claim superiority over another, because all are frail and have acted in an inappropriate manner at one time or another. In America the flag represents the knowledge of equality, so that prejudice will be looked at as evil. The flag states we are all equal in original creation. Every one of us has fingerprints that identify us as individually different, but we cannot be construed as being better than someone else. Under the banner of the flag of the United State of America, no entity or person should be allowed to prosper if they discriminate against another American. If and when it is discovered that discrimination has occurred, the government that was created for the people and by the people should order that American flag to be taken down and the facility closed, because the flag itself testifies against their actions. So it is of great importance for us as Americans to understand without reservation that regardless of our individual prominence, we are equal in our human will and freedom.

If the government of America wishes to have a stable economy forever, it must enforce equal rights for all of it citizens to be employed. Employment for all citizens is good, because it eliminates or lessens the financial burden on the government. When citizens work, the economy grows, and this creates more jobs. A stable economy is dependent upon every citizen being employed. When people are employed they pay taxes, which helps to eradicate the federal deficit. When people are employed, it helps to reduce crime in society overall. It helps people maintain better and cleaner neighborhoods. It helps reduce long-term illnesses, because most places of employment offer some type of health insurance. The more money a person makes the less the government will spend toward the individual's welfare. When Hurricane Katrina hit Louisiana, Mississippi, and the gulf of Alabama, the cost to the government was scaled down because Americans, rich and poor, gave out of their pockets, which ultimately decreased the amount that otherwise would have been paid by the Federal Emergency Management Agency (FEMA).

If affirmative action plans are the only way to make mainstream corporate America adhere to fair hiring practices, then the federal government must enforce and encourage this plan for the sake of the economy. It must be one of the Department of Labor's primary objectives, because everyone that is capable of working should not be denied employment based on their color and gender. The only reform that gets people off of government subsidies is equality in the work place. God has blessed America; now America must bless God by showing unity.

"God Bless America"
By Irving Berlin

God bless America, Land that I love.
Stand beside her, And guide her,
Thru the night with a light from above.

~ ~ ~

From the mountains, To the prairies,
To the oceans white with foam.
God bless America, My home, sweet, home,

~ ~ ~

God bless America, My home, sweet, home

Conclusion

The flag of the United States of America is the embodiment of the law of liberty found in the Constitution. Everyone cannot understand nor have access to the written document. For this reason the flag is flown for all to see the liberty the Constitution grants to every citizen. The flag is the symbol of freedom for all that enter legally in America's gates, and also extends protection to illegal aliens. Whether we came here on the ships of Columbus, the ships of the Pilgrims, the ships of the slave masters, the ships of migration, or on broken pieces, the flag gives us hope.

This is a great country, and we are free. Our women can get an education, they can be educators, and they can become leaders and instruct men, women, and children. They can even be nominated for the presidency of the United States. With enough votes they can become president.

Our enemies hate us for being free. They hate us because each citizen has a voice in what goes on. They hate us because the Lord God of heaven blesses us. They hate us because we are friends and the sister of Israel. The Lord said, "I will bless them that bless you [Israel] and curse them that curse you." We are blessed people. We have almost everything that will satisfy the heart. We even have the smartest and the brightest from other countries that have become citizens of this great country. We have people from across the globe knocking our doors down to get in. No other nation has this. We are black, white, brown, red, and yellow. We are Americans. Our flag forces legislative leaders to be honest or suffer the consequences of punishment for prejudicial treatment of any citizen. Our political system of checks and balances is one of the greatest in the world and will protect each citizen from civil injustice.

(1) The Holy Bible
(2) The Preamble
(3) The Constitution
(4) The Bill of Rights
(5) The Status of Liberty

So, my dear fellow Americans, we are all under the same flag. Individually and collectively, we can fight for our rights. Things are not prefect, but they are much better than they were because God and "Old Glory" have fought for us. We cannot separate God from the flag. We cannot separate the flag from God. The government is here because of God, and this flag is here because of God. America is the Promised Land. The flag is the light that leads to victory. The issue is not what color we are; it is what color the flag is. So, it is a Red, White, and Blue issue.

END NOTES

[1] *Hastings Dictionary of the Bible* (1969).

[2] The chart "The Illustrious Lineage of the Royal House of Britain" may be purchased through Dolores Press, Glendale, California.

[3] Graphic of the Great Seal accessed from *www.americana.ru/AboutUSA-seal.htm*. This picture is in the public domain.

[4] This graphic of the Great Seal is in the public domain.

[5] Sharon Turner, "The History of the Anglo-Saxons from the Earliest Period to the Norman Conquest," Encyclopedia Britannica. Accessed from *www.soundchristian.com*. Apocrypha 2, Esdras 13, Josephus, and the Declaration of Arbroath 1320.

[6] *The New Book of Knowledge*, Wikipedia, the free online encyclopedia. Accessed from *www.wikipedia.org*.

[7] Etching in "Antonio de Herrerra y Tordesillas, History General de las Indias Occidentales" (1728). Reproduction number LC-USZ62-8390, Library of Congress.

[8] Reproduction number LC-USZ62-8355, page 63, Library of Congress.

[9] Albert Henry Newman, *The Manual of Church History,* vols. 1 and 2 (1899).

[10] Albert Henry Newman, *The Manual of Church History,* vol. 1 (1899), 537.

[11] B. K. Kuper, *The Church in History* (Christian School International, 1982), 162.

[12] *The New Book of Knowledge* (Grolier, Inc., 1988).

[13] *The New Book of Knowledge* (Grolier, Inc., 1988).

[14] "The Africans of the Slave Bark *Wildfire,*" *Harper's Weekly* page 344. This excerpt was from the journal of a ship captain as he examined the black African slaves. Used by permission from *Son of the South.net.*

[15] *The New Book of Knowledge* (Grolier, Inc., 1988).

[16] Franklin Rutledge. [2005, Sermon: God is Faithful.]

[17] Anonymous –Email from Candace Ramirez

[18] "Voices from the Days of Slavery" Sound Recording. Library of Congress afc99999001/t9990a.

[19] *Ibid.*

[20] National Archives and Records Administration. Accessed from *Slavetreatment.jpe* (67KB, MIME type: image/jpeg.

[21] Library of Congress, LC-USZ62-2582.

[22] Book and Special Collections Division, Library of Congress, LC-USZ62-10293.

[23] "The Circle of Knowledge," 1936, Encyclopedia Britannica, Wikipedia, the free online Encyclopedia. Accessed from *www. wikipedia.org.*

[24] "The Circle of Knowledge," Encyclopedia Britannica, page 703. Accessed from *www.wikipedia.org.*

[25] Compare with Josephus, Book V, 6:4-5.

[26] Marc Arkin, "The Federalist Brief" 04-22. Accessed from *www. earstohear.net.*

[27] *American Heritage* American History. Marshall B. Davidson. American Heritage Pub. Co.; Distribution by Simon and Schuster [1968].

[28] From George Washington's first Inaugural Address.

[29] Prints and Photographs Division, Library of Congress, LC-USZ62-5780.

[30] It is known that Ross made flags for the navy of Pennsylvania, but there is no firm evidence in support of this story about our nation's flag.

[31] Multimedia Edition, Encyclopedia Britannica CD99 (1998).

[32] Call number: Lot 4703; Reproduction number: LC-USZC4-2998; Library of Congress, created and published USZ6-875.

[33] The National Flag Day Foundation, Inc.

[34] Accessed from *Crime Library.com.*

[35] *Webster's New Collegiate Dictionary* (G & C Marriam Company, 1979).

[36] Lerone Bennett, "Before the Mayflower," PBS. Accessed at *www.afro.com.* Information also derived from Encyclopedia Britannica, World Books, and *Biography.com.,* Wikipedia, the free online Encyclopedia at *www.wikipedia.org..*

[37] National Archives of Historical Records.

[38] Rare Book Collection, University of North Carolina at Chapel Hill; Call number E449; W442 (1839).

[39] John Hope Franklin, Emancipation Proclamation: January 1, 1863. Washington, D.C.: National Archives and Records Administration, 1994.

[40] Library of Congress: LC-USZ62-1287.

[41] Library of Congress: LC-USZ62-36161; Call number: PC/US-1861.A000.

[42] "Voices from the Days of Slavery." Sound Recording. Library of Congress.

[43] Robert Wallace, *The Genesis Factor* (William Morrow & Company, 1979).

[44] Doug Linder, "Armistad Trials," Famous American Trials. Accessed at *www.law.umkc.edu.*

[45] Prints and Photographs Division, Library of Congress; LC-DIG ppmsc-01269 original.

References

All Scriptures are taken from the New King James Version. Copyright © 1979, 1980, 1982 by Thomas Nelson, Inc. Used by permission. All rights reserved.

American Park Network

Armstrong, Herbert W., *Britain and the United States in Prophecy* (World Wide Church of God, 1980).

Bartleman, Frank, *Azusa Street* (Logos International, 1980).

Brinkley, Douglas, *History of the United States* (American Heritage).

EnchantedLearning.com

Johnson, Willis F., *A History of the Nation's Flag* (1930).

Krythe, Maymie R., *What So Proudly We Hail* (Harper & Row, 1968).

Kuper, B. K., *The Church in History* (Christian School International, 1982).

Library of Congress Archives–photos

New Book of Knowledge, The (Grolier, Inc., 1988).

New Encyclopedia Britannica, The (1988).

Newcombe, Nora, *Child Development (change over time)* (Harper Collins Collet Publishing, 1996).

Newman, Albert Henry, *The Manual of Church History*, vols. 1 and 2 (1899).

Sanders, Rufus, G. W., Ph.D., *William Joseph Seymour* (Alexandria Publications, 2001).

Schauffler, Robert H., *Our Flag in Verse and Prose* (Moffat, Year, and Company, 1976).

Seifert, Hoffnung, and Hoffnung, *Life Span and Development* (Houghton Mifflin Company, 2000).

"Statue of Liberty," American Park Network.

"Statue of Liberty," National Achieves Historical Records.

(Includepicture\d"../images/c..barthold.jpg"_).

"Statue of Liberty," *NPS Historical Handbook.*

Strong's Exhaustive Concordance of the Bible (Holman Bible Publishers, 1996).

Wallace, Robert, *The Genesis Factor* (William Morrow & Company, 1979).

Webster's New Collegiate Dictionary (G & C Merriam Company, 1979).

Zinn, Howard, *People's History of the United States* (HarperCollins, 1999).

GLOSSARY OF TERMS

Development: Orderly and relatively enduring changes over time in physical and neurological structures, in thought processes, in emotions, in forms of social interaction, and in many other behaviors.

Devotion: Ardent love or affection.

Expect: To consider probable or certain.

Indentured Servitude: This began in North American with the founding of the colonies, and existed concurrently with free labor and slavery until the American Revolution. Its subjects were males and females of Western European (mainly British) origin. The terms of indentured servitude were contingent upon the strength of the individual's position, and the preferences of his master. The harshest terms and longest indentures were imposed upon criminals whose death sentences (often for political offenses and numerous crimes now regarded as misdemeanors) were commutable upon entering into colonial indentures. At the other extreme, those able to negotiate the terms of indenture were able to obtain contracts generally patterned after English apprenticeship customs and were usually free after five to seven years of service. Colonial laws gave some protection to the indentured servant but also sanctioned and enforced performance of the contract whether oral or written.

Promise: A legally binding declaration that gives the person to whom it is made a right to expect or to claim the performance or forbearance of a specified act; grounds for expectation.

Slave: One who is owned by another and deprived of most of all rights and freedoms, hence the term chattel slave, denoting personal property at law. The slave is dependent on the whim of the owner, who may generally force him to do any service and, at least in principle, may usually even dispose of his life.

Slavery: A system that embraces different degrees of social status. Slaves in ancient Rome, for instance, could be educated and could, in many cases, acquire property and the means of buying their freedom. The law expressly forbade the black Africans in Southern United States to have these rights.

ACKNOWLEDGEMENTS

Most books cannot be written without the assistance of others. I would like to thank some special people for assisting me in small ways but extremely valuable to me. Michele Sumecki, Angela Daniels for their invaluable assistance in the area of etymology. Ellen DePaola for her assistance with computer formatting and other Word applications. To Jocelyn Stewart for her timely and descriptive poem.

Thanks to Praez Media for their sound professional guidance. You helped me through what would have been a book full of information without structure. Without you the book would have been syntactically messy.

Thanks to the many people that encouraged me to continue with this type of work. Thanks to some special people that supported me financially: Sandra Watts, Myra Wimberly, Anita Jackson, Edward Thomas Jr, Ruby Watkins, Terry Rutledge, Michael Fazzino, Freddie Spikes, Shirley Nichols, Jerry Aplegrin, Linda Ligon, Henry Robinson, Alberta Robertson, Carol Smith, Addie Strickland, Larry King, Mary Fulgham and others that wished to remained anonymous. Without your financial help this manuscript would have never been made into a book.

Thanks to Patricia Bollmann (Florissant, MO) for her help in editing this manuscript. You are God sent. You truly have made this book much better to read.

ABOUT THE AUTHOR

Franklin Edward Rutledge. Born in the town of Wilton, Alabama. The sixth of twelve children from the deceased parents of Forrest Freeman Rutledge and Ola Mae Rutledge. He is an ordained elder of the Pentecostal Assemblies of the World, Inc. He is married to Shiann Rutledge. They have three children: F. Tyrell, F. Michael and Jessica Jacinda Rutledge. He served 4 years in the United States Military (Navy). He's currently studying psychology at Central Connecticut State University as a part time student. He is dedicated to the true interpretation of God's word.

www.ingramcontent.com/pod-product-compliance
Lightning Source LLC
Chambersburg PA
CBHW061345280526
45784CB00001B/137